Strength, Support, Setbacks and Solutions

The developmental pathway to addiction recovery

David Best

Pavilion

Strength, Support, Setbacks and Solutions: A developmental pathway to addiction recovery

Published by:
Pavilion Publishing and Media Ltd
Rayford House
School Road
Hove
East Sussex
BN3 5HX
Tel: 01273 434 943
Fax: 01273 227 308
Email: info@pavpub.com

Published 2014

A catalogue record for this book is available from the British Library.

Print ISBN: 978-1-908993-47-2   EPDF: 978-1-909810-75-4
EPUB: 978-1-909810-76-1   MOBI: 978-1-909810-77-8

Pavilion is the leading training and development provider and publisher in the health, social care and allied fields, providing a range of innovative training solutions underpinned by sound research and professional values. We aim to put our customers first, through excellent customer service and value.

Author: David Best
Production editor: Catherine Ansell-Jones, Pavilion Publishing and Media Ltd
Cover design: Phil Morash, Pavilion Publishing and Media Ltd
Page layout and typesetting: Anthony Pitt, Pavilion Publishing and Media Ltd
Printing: Ashford Colour Press

This book is dedicated to the memory of James Best, my father, who passed away on the 8th of February 2013. The delay in producing this book was a result of the pain and loss I felt. I miss you and I will always love you.

Contents

About the author

David Best is head of research and workforce development at Turning Point and associate professor in addiction studies at Monash University in Melbourne. He leads the treatment and systems team at Turning Point, and is course co-ordinator for the new Masters in Addictive Behaviour at Monash University. He is also chair of Recovery Academy Australia and on the advisory board of the Recovery Research Institute.

David is a qualified psychologist and criminologist, and has worked in both research and policy areas for around 20 years. He has worked and studied at Strathclyde University (Glasgow), the Institute of Psychiatry, London School of Economics, the University of Birmingham, the University of the West of Scotland, and Monash University. He has held research policy roles at the Police Complaints Authority and the National Treatment Agency for Substance Misuse.

David is the author of *Mapping the Road to Addiction Recovery* (2012) and *Addiction Recovery* (2012) and has written more than 140 peer-reviewed journal papers. His main area of interest is around pathways to recovery and the role of social networks in promoting well-being.

Acknowledgements

I would like to acknowledge many friends and colleagues who have supported me in producing this book, including my colleagues at Turning Point in Melbourne, in the Recovery Academy in both the UK and Australia, and many, many people who have shown me what an amazing thing recovery is and what incredible people it produces. And a further thank you to all of those who have contributed to this book as research subjects, critical friends and colleagues.

About the book

This book is a natural follow-up to *Addiction Recovery: A movement for social change and personal growth in the UK* (Best, 2012) and tests a number of the hypotheses and models outlined in that book. The work presented here continues to focus on alcohol and illicit drug addiction – with an increasing focus on the unique experiences of addiction professionals who are themselves in recovery. This is a particularly important theme as this is a group whose experiences and interests have not been adequately addressed in the recovery literature (or indeed in the wider addictions research literature), and who have had to make a range of decisions about the disclosure of their addiction status in terms of both their personal and professional lives.

This will be embedded within an emerging developmental and social identity model of recovery that continues the themes presented in *Addiction Recovery* (Best, 2012). The primary tenets of this model are that:

- Recovery is a gradual process of emergence and change.
- This involves the growth of a new identity that develops in the context of a changing social network and involves the emergence of a new socially mediated identity.
- This identity may have a 'recovery identity' as a central part of it but this is not necessary. However, it is extremely unlikely that the new identity will involve going back to being the same person that the individual was before their period of active addiction.
- This transition is often framed as 'just being normal' in the sense of the predominance of everyday concerns over those that were predominant during the period of active addiction.
- Nonetheless, the skills and resources that are acquired or honed during the recovery journey (recovery capital) will provide the person in recovery with a unique set of skills and supports for that ongoing life journey.

This book uses a variety of existing and original research data to illustrate aspects of that process with the same primary emphasis on the importance of others, the importance of families and communities, and the recognition that people in recovery are an incredible source of hope and optimism not only for those in active addiction, but as assets in their communities who can inspire and sustain enormous social change.

Overview of the book

Chapter 1 provides a brief introduction to the concept of recovery and its origins in the mutual aid group movement and the recovery movement in mental health. It picks up on a number of the themes in *Addiction Recovery* (Best, 2012).

Chapter 2 outlines the theoretical model for the book based on a developmental model of growth in recovery capital linked to social change and networks. The key to this model is the idea that individuals achieve recovery as a gradual process of growth and identity change that is mediated by social supports.

Chapter 3 starts with a review and a re-analysis of the Glasgow Recovery Study (Best *et al*, 2011 a, b), in which the initial model of recovery as well-being was framed based on the importance of connectedness to others in recovery and their role in initiating and supporting meaningful activities.

Chapter 4 provides an initial summary of recovery stories from a pilot study undertaken in Melbourne in 2013 in which individuals provided online responses about their recovery journeys. This provides a brief summary of the developmental model and its relationship to the constructions of recovery identities for people at different stages of their own recovery journey.

Chapter 5 outlines the rationale for the main study. The importance of the recovery experiences and stories of professionals in the addiction field is described and conceptualised in terms of the developmental model and a new concept, that of recovery disclosure and its impact on the journey, is outlined.

Chapter 6 provides a qualitative account of the key stages of the recovery experiences of the professionals in the field based on a number of case studies in which individual stories are relayed in some detail to illustrate key aspects of the recovery journey.

Chapter 7 outlines the developmental pathways of professionals in recovery. Using the Lifetime Drug Use History to provide a timeline method, this chapter shows both the consistencies and the variabilities in the recovery pathways across a range of professionals in recovery.

Chapter 8 reviews the well-being and life satisfaction of the professional groups in the context of comparison samples of other recovery populations (in terms of recovery capital) and in terms of treatment populations for the relevant sub-scales.

Chapter 9 reframes the developmental recovery model in the light of the new data and recent theoretical developments in the addiction recovery movement. The developmental social identity model is presented in this chapter.

Chapter 10 reviews the key findings presented in this book. It links to both the current situation in the addictions field in the UK and internationally, and also looks to the future and the opportunities for building a recovery movement that transcends areas as diverse as social work, criminology and mental health.

References

Best D, Gow J, Taylor A, Knox T, Groshkova T & White W (2011a) Mapping the recovery stories of drinkers and drug users in Glasgow: quality of life and its associations with measures of recovery capital. *Drug and Alcohol Review* **31** (3) 334–341.

Best D, Gow J, Taylor A, Knox T & White W (2011b) Reccovery from heroin or alcohol dependence: a qualitative account of the recovery experience in Glasgow. *Journal of Drug Issues* **11** (1) 359–378.

Best D (2012) *Addiction Recovery: A movement for social change and personal growth in the UK.* Brighton: Pavilion Publishing.

Chapter 1: Recovery – a personal journey of change and hope

The definition trap

In both Scotland and England (Scottish Government, 2008; HM Government, 2010) the current drug policies show a strong commitment towards recovery as a new philosophy to addressing a significant social problem, based on a model of hope and change that has spawned a social movement in both countries. This has resulted in the growth of recovery oversight organisations and the emergence of local policies that strive to encourage and support personal recovery from alcohol and drug problems. This transition has its origins in part in the success of the recovery movement in the mental health field but also in the user empowerment and involvement model, and in a transdisciplinary switch to a focus on strengths and on communities.

A major component of the challenge of advancing the recovery movement has been how elusive recovery has been to characterise and define. In the forerunner to this work, *Addiction Recovery: A movement for social change and personal growth in the UK* (Best, 2012) defines recovery as a *'sense of hope, a sense of purpose, and sense of belonging and a positive identity'*. This contrasts with the more diagnostic definitions that have resulted from the major consensus expert groups in the US and in the UK. In the US, the expert group agreed upon *'A voluntarily maintained lifestyle characterised by sobriety, personal health and citizenship'* (Betty Ford Institute Consensus Panel, 2007, p222), with the subsequent UK definition from the UK Drug Policy Commission (UKDPC) broadly similar in both scope and composition: *'Voluntarily sustained control over substance use which maximises health and well-being and participation in the rights, roles and responsibilities of society'* (UK Drug Policy Commission, 2008, p6).

There are two problems with these definitions – how they are operationalised and crucially by whom. In contrast, in the context of mental health recovery,

Patricia Deegan argues that: '*Recovery refers to the lived experience of people as they accept and overcome the challenge of disability ... they experience themselves as recovering a new sense of self and of purpose within and beyond the limits of the disability*'. More recently, and describing the emergence of the recovery movement in Connecticut, Valentine (2011) describes how various inclusion criteria (sobriety, commitment, etc.) were attempted and discarded in favour of a classification that '*you are in recovery if you say you are*'.

While personal ownership of recovery is a critical component in a social movement that attempts to move away from the primacy of the clinician or expert in determining who is in recovery and when, it is much less helpful to the researcher attempting to measure prevalence rates of recovery and related characteristics, or the commissioner or policy maker attempting to assess whether someone is in recovery or not. One of the major challenges the recovery field faces is the criticism that it is too vague and based on wishful thinking, with few clear specific actions or recommendations for clinicians or policy-makers. So the following sections of this chapter will try to address some fundamental questions about the recovery movement:

- Where does it come from?
- Is there any evidence that it works?
- Why is it any different to what services have always done to help people?
- Is there a price to pay for a recovery agenda in terms of loss or damage to established and cherished methods and treatment programmes?

A brief summary of the origins of the recovery movement

While there have been a number of influential abstinence and temperance movements (outlined in William White's *Slaying the Dragon: The history of addiction treatment and recovery in America* (1998)), there are four key historical threads in the emergence of the recovery movement in the UK. The first is the powerful presence and support of the mutual aid movement, particularly the 12-step fellowships, that have formed the long-standing foundations for peer, community-based support and the parallel evolution of the therapeutic community movement, with its focus on 'right living'. The second is the mental health recovery movement, particularly strong in Australia and Scotland in terms of direct influence on the recovery movement in alcohol and other drugs. The third key inspiration and source has been the recovery movement in the US and the writings of key inspirational figures, while the fourth is around the user and carer empowerment movement that has emerged in a number of countries but which has been particularly influential in the US and the UK and which has driven forward policy and practice.

1. The mutual aid movement and the therapeutic communities

From the first meeting of Bill Wilson and Dr Bob in Akron, Ohio, in 1935 to the publication of the first edition of 'The Big Book' in 1939, there has been an explosion of the mutual aid network based on the 12 steps and the 12 traditions, and variants on the original Alcoholics' Anonymous (AA) model as the fellowship has gathered support in specific groups for narcotics, for cocaine, and for an increasing number of process addictions that do not involve the ingestion of psychoactive substances. In the UK, AA meetings have grown from the first meeting in 1947 to more than 4,300 local groups. Other 12-step groups have also spread throughout the UK, with more than 600 local Narcotics Anonymous (NA) meetings (Lopez-Gaston *et al*, 2010), and at the time of writing there are around 800 meetings listed on the NA website. Cocaine Anonymous (CA) groups are also rapidly growing in the UK. A recent survey in the UK indicated that in 2011 there were approximately 4,600 AA meetings, 896 NA meetings, 90 Al-Anon meetings, 242 CA meetings and 88 SMART Recovery meetings (McCartney, personal communication, 2012).

So what is it that mutual aid groups do that can provide lessons for the recovery models under construction in the UK? International longitudinal outcome studies consistently identify that participation in mutual aid is associated with increased long-term recovery rates and improved overall functioning, as well as reduction in drug-related costs to society (Kelly & Yeterian, 2008; White, 2009a, 2009b).More recent research has focused not just on attendance at mutual aid meetings but involvement in groups themselves as well as the activities suggested by these groups, such as helping set up meetings, reading literature, getting a sponsor and working the steps. Broadly these studies show that the higher the 'dose' of involvement, the better the outcomes (Donovan & Floyd, 2008). Improving engagement with mutual aid groups is a highly cost-effective strategy as accessing these voluntary-run programmes is virtually cost-free and, as a professional aftercare intervention, there is a distinct benefit for the maintenance of treatment gains with attendance of mutual aid groups (Humphreys, 2004). Post-treatment 12-step participation is a strong predictor of long-term abstinence, especially when participation is initiated early on in the recovery journey (Gossop *et al*, 2003).

Recent research has started to identify the key elements of mutual aid participation that may promote recovery. Litt *et al* (2007a) conducted a randomised trial to predict the longevity of abstinence in a group of drinkers completing residential detoxification. The study assessed the impact of standard case management compared to network support, where the latter attempted to add one sober person to the former drinker's social network. This led to highly significant improvements in abstinence rates with the authors concluding that the addition of one clean and sober individual to the social network reduced relapse rates in drinkers by 27% in the following year (Litt *et al*, 2007b). The effect achieved is much greater than would be achieved from most treatment-based aftercare interventions.

In the second key study, Timko *et al* (2005) conducted a randomised control trial to compare a 'standard' and 'intensive' referral intervention to encourage 12-step meeting attendance among substance misusing outpatients. At six months, those in the intensive referral condition showed significantly greater 12-step involvement (for example, they accessed a provided service, experienced a spiritual awakening and currently had a sponsor) and achieved significantly better substance use outcomes. So what are the key implications of these two studies? It is essential that there are effective bridges built from formal treatment to recovery groups and communities, and that by adding sober individuals to the social network of former users, there is increased sober socialisation that generates key supports and resources for ongoing sobriety. This social theme will persist in the discussion of the mental health recovery movement that follows.

However, it would be remiss to discuss the origins of recovery within the alcohol and drug field without considering the second primary recovery community – one that has grown up around the therapeutic community (TC) model in the UK, summarised in George De Leon's *Therapeutic Community: Theory, model and method* (2000). Malivert *et al* (2012) conducted a systematic review of TC effectiveness (based on 12 studies of community TCs) and noted that completion rates varied widely (9–56%). All the studies included in the review demonstrated a decrease in substance use at follow-up, although between one-fifth and one-third of residents re-entered treatment during the follow-up period. Although there were methodological variations across studies, TC treatment retention and completion were identified as the most robust predictors of abstinence at follow-up (Malivert *et al*, 2012).

What is critical in the recovery context is that the TC model involves immersion in the community to bring about an identity change that will enable long-term transition to meaningful recovery that can be sustained in the community. TCs are a recognised and publicly-funded treatment resource in both the UK and Australia and are often seen as a treatment of last resort for some of the most problematic clients who may have 'failed' in all other treatment services. The key aspects of the TC model is that they have a very strong peer and community component, the model sees addictive behaviours as only symptomatic of deeper problems and that the solutions arise from peer and community learning and growth. De Leon discusses this process in identity terms as '*dissipation of old identity elements, restructuring elements of new social and personal identities during treatment and continued identity development beyond treatment in the real world*' (2000, p345). In some ways, the TC environment is the perfect location for studying identity change in recovery as it is rare as a treatment modality that actively pursues identity change as a core goal of treatment.

2.   The mental health recovery movement

A key 'expert by experience' in the mental health field, Pat Deegan, has argued that '*Recovery is a process, not an endpoint or destination. Recovery is an attitude, a way of approaching the day and the challenges I face … I know I have certain limitations and things I can't do. But rather than letting these limitations be occasions for despair and giving up, I have learned that in knowing what I can't do, I also open up the possibilities of all I can do*' (1993, p7). This is critical to the idea that recovery is not just about overcoming symptoms and 'beating' the disease but is about a profound change of thinking in how we characterise recovery.

In testing this model in the alcohol and other drugs (AOD) space, Hibbert and Best (2011) found evidence of a 'better than well' phenomenon in which those in long-term recovery showed higher levels of quality of life (significantly for dimensions assessing social and environmental life quality) than the comparison group of the general public who had never been addicted. Why this is important for a recovery movement is two-fold – first, that recovery is not about going back to some imaginary pre-symptomatic state, but is more typically characterised by resilience and growth and moving beyond the 'sickness' paradigm of medicine to an altered state of meaning and purpose that transcends symptom reduction. Second, this study implies the existence of a body of people in recovery who are 'better than well' who, as a consequence, are the living embodiment of recovery success and so are its most likely 'transmitters'. In other words, one of the key lessons from the mental health recovery model is that it focuses less on cure and more on life quality and purpose. The Hibbert and Best (2011) study also identifies a cohort of individuals who are icons of what is possible in recovery, for others to observe, learn from and imitate.

In a UK context, Repper and Perkins (2003) have argued that: *'Recovery is not a professional intervention, like medication or therapy, and mental health workers do not hold the key. Many people have described the enormous support they have received from others who have faced a similar challenge...'* (Repper & Perkins, 2003, p47). This notion of recovery as something that happens outside of treatment was further promoted in Slade's (2009) claim that *'The goal of mental health services is more explicitly the promotion and support of personal recovery. Clinical recovery has value, as one approach to supporting personal recovery. However, a primary focus on personal recovery would fundamentally change the values, goals and working practices of mental health services'.*

In addition to the arguments by parallel, the mental health recovery movement has also provided an evidence base for recovery models and approaches that have tackled some professional scepticisms and vested interests. A key summary article in *The Psychiatrist* by Warner (2010), reviewing the evidence for recovery from over 100 studies, concluded that 20% of schizophrenics make a complete recovery and 40% a 'social recovery' (defined as economic and residential independence and low social disruption), with work and empowerment two of the key features of the recovery process. Harding *et al* (1987) conducted a 32-year follow-up study of the most difficult-to-place third of a population of psychiatric inpatient residents – at the follow-up point 81% were able to look after themselves, 25% were fully recovered and 41% showed significant improvements, while only 11% of people with severe and enduring mental illness did not show any improvement and remained within the treatment and support system.

In 2011, Leamy *et al* published the first systematic review and narrative synthesis of mental health recovery papers, including a total of 97 papers in the final review. They identified 13 characteristics of the recovery journey including recovery as an individual and unique process; recovery as a journey; recovery as gradual and life-changing; as supported by a healing and supportive environment; and as something that can take place without professional assistance. They also identified five key recovery processes – connectedness; hope and optimism about the future; identity; meaning in life; and empowerment, that form the basis for the acronym 'CHIME' as a summary of the key elements of effective recovery programmes. Their model also suggested a stage model and a specific approach for cultural and minority groups. The authors concluded that a clear and evidence-based conceptual framework was potentially beneficial in developing a clear taxonomy system and research agenda for recovery.

This evidence base has been highly influential in persuading policy makers of the merits of a recovery approach, with particular resonance on the emergence of the recovery model as the driving force for the AOD strategy in Scotland. The 2008 drug strategy in Scotland, *The Road to Recovery* (Scottish Government, 2008), makes very explicit this link: *'Recovery as an achievable goal is a concept pioneered in recent years with great success in the field of mental health. The Scottish Recovery Network has been raising awareness of the fact that people can and do recover from even the most serious and long-term mental health problem'* (p23). The lineage is made clear in the action specified on the following page of the strategy that *'we will establish and support a Drug Recovery Network [later named the Scottish Drugs Recovery Consortium] along the lines of the Scottish Recovery Network'* (Scottish Government, 2008, p24). In other words, the perceived success of the recovery movement in mental health has been a strong component of the will to generate an equivalent movement for the AOD field. While the English strategy makes no explicit reference to the mental health recovery movement, the definition provided of recovery as *'an individual, person-centred journey, as opposed to an end state, and one that will mean different things to different people'* (HM Government, 2010, p18) has strong echoes of the definitions offered by Deegan and by Repper and Perkins.

The other significant contribution of the mental health recovery movement has been in the area of peer-based interventions and empowerment. Thus, the delivery of Pathways to Recovery reported significant increases in self-esteem, self-efficacy, social support and spiritual well-being in individuals with serious mental illness (Fukui *et al*, 2010) with evidence that peer delivery of the intervention was also highly effective (Barbic *et al*, 2009). More recently, evaluations of the Building Recovery of Individual Dreams and Goals through Education and Support (BRIDGES) over eight peer-delivered sessions led to significant improvements in recovery and hopefulness among individuals with severe mental illness. In other words, peer interventions have a crucial role to play in supporting ongoing recovery pathways.

One of the key areas of direct overlap is around co-occurring mental health and addiction problems – referred to as dual diagnosis. While this will be a key theme in Chapter 10 as we look to how the recovery movement will move forward, the struggle to manage co-occurring disorders in acute treatment services may offer an opportunity for the recovery movement to bridge the ongoing divide between mental health and addiction treatment services through working in the community to support individuals to engage in recovery activities and to support and promote their recovery journeys.

3.   The US recovery movement

The date of emergence of a recovery 'movement' in the US is difficult to pin down and there are some powerful and charismatic leaders of the recovery movement that have emerged, but probably none more powerful than William White whose prodigious research output can be viewed at http://www.williamwhitepapers. com. This body of research has not only documented the emergence of a recovery movement beyond the 12-step mutual aid groups, it has also brought together a range of evidence that has been powerful in convincing service commissioners and politicians of the centrality of the recovery paradigm and approach.

Kelly and White have brought together much of this evidence in the edited book *Addiction Recovery Management* (2011), where the research evidence for individual recovery is not only summarised but there is also a section of five chapters reviewing systemic approaches to recovery, including chapters on the emergence of a recovery-oriented system of care in three US sites – Chicago, Connecticut and Philadelphia. White has also published a series of monographs that combine a history of recovery activity with concise summaries of the evidence, which are seminal documents in constructing evidence-based foundations for a recovery approach (eg. White, 2008; White, 2009b).

A further summary of the evidence was undertaken by Sheedy and Whitter (2009) for the Substance Abuse and Mental Health Services Administration, entitled *Guiding Principles and Elements of Recovery-Oriented Systems of Care: What do we know from the research?*. In addition to creating a definition of recovery as '*A process of change through which an individual achieves abstinence and improved health, wellness and quality of life*' (Sheedy & Whitter, 2009, p1), it also goes on to define what the core principles are for recovery-oriented systems of care. There are 17 such principles. The system should:

1. be person-centred
2. be inclusive of family and other ally involvement
3. have individualised and comprehensive services across the lifespan
4. have systems anchored in the community
5. provide a system that offers continuity of care
6. provide partnership-consultant relationships
7. be strength-based
8. be culturally responsive
9. be responsive to personal belief systems

10. be committed to peer recovery support services

11. include the voices and experiences of recovering individuals and their families

12. provide integrated services

13. provide system-wide education and training

14. provide ongoing monitoring and outreach

15. be outcomes driven

16. be research based

17. be adequately and flexibly financed.

Further, Sheedy and Whitter (2009) summarised the evidence on the epidemiology of recovery concluding that, on average, the epidemiological evidence would suggest that 58% of people with a chronic substance dependence achieve sustained recovery, although the rates reported in individual studies range from 30–72%.

Following a significant community consultation, the Substance Abuse and Mental Health Services Administration (SAMHSA) has reached the following position and has delineated four major dimensions that support a life in recovery:

1. **Health:** overcoming or managing one's disease(s) as well as living in a physically and emotionally healthy way.

2. **Home:** a stable and safe place to live.

3. **Purpose:** meaningful daily activities, such as a job, school, volunteerism, family caretaking, or creative endeavors, and the independence, income and resources to participate in society.

4. **Community:** relationships and social networks that provide support, friendship, love, and hope.

SAMHSA also oversees 'Recovery Month' as a joint activity that *'promotes the societal benefits of prevention, treatment, and recovery for substance use and mental disorders, celebrates people in recovery, lauds the contributions of treatment and service providers, and promotes the message that recovery in all its forms is possible'* (SAMHSA, 2014). The role of SAMHSA in legitimising recovery has had its greatest vindication in a Presidential Proclamation by Barack Obama, in which he stated:

'The journey to recovery requires great fortitude and a supportive network. As we celebrate National Alcohol and Drug Addiction Recovery Month, we also express our appreciation for the family members, mutual aid groups, peer support programs, health professionals, and community leaders that provide compassion, care, and

hope. Across America, we must spread the word that substance abuse is preventable, that addiction is treatable and that recovery is possible.' (Obama, 2010)

The politicisation of recovery has been driven by a grassroots network of activities and recovery communities that have communicated through a range of online networks, particularly Faces and Voices of Recovery (FAVOR) (http://www.facesandvoicesofrecovery.org). FAVOR is a national network of over 20,000 individuals and organisations joining together to speak out and support local, state, regional and national recovery advocacy by being a national rallying point for recovery advocates; linking advocates to organising, policy, and research support; building advocacy skills through hands-on training and technical assistance; and improving access to policymakers and the media. FAVOR developed the first 'Recovery Bill of Rights' and has focused on the provision of information, on challenging discrimination and the development of advocacy networks.

The Americans have also built alliances and relationships with their UK equivalents to support and enable recovery activities. A number of major US recovery advocates have come to the UK to speak (William White, Phil Valentine, Pat Taylor) or, in the case of Keith Humphreys, come to advise on policy. The legitimacy and mainstream status of the US recovery movement has been a major source of hope and inspiration in the UK.

However, the final word in this section will go to a recent review article by Humphreys and Lembke (2013). They argue that there are three prime sources of data that challenge the assumption that there is only a weak and optimistic evidence base around recovery. They argue that the evidence for a recovery approach is extremely convincing in three areas – around recovery housing, around the mutual aid movement and around peer-based interventions. In the latter area, they provide a strong support for both the added benefit that peer interventions provide as a supplement to acute addiction treatment, but they also argue that peer-delivered interventions are supported as a standalone intervention. The article is critical in its direct challenge to recovery critics by identifying three areas where there is strong empirical evidence – including but not restricted to randomised trials. This is critical in helping to direct our future endeavours around an evidence-based and robust model for recovery interventions.

4. User involvement and user participation

This has its origins partly in the mental health recovery movement but extends more widely than this to an increasing evidence base suggesting that peers can have a significant role to play in the development of services and in the delivery of interventions. Indeed, this is one of the areas of clear consistency and overlap between the harm reduction and recovery movements – the centrality of user involvement and participation although the two have differed markedly in the framing of this user participation!

As characterised by Humphreys and Lembke (2013), there is a supportive evidence base around peer-based therapeutic activities. A randomised trial conducted by Galanter *et al* (1987), which compared entirely professionally-led treatment programmes with professional and peer co-led treatment programmes, reported no difference in substance use outcomes, and superior social adjustment among patients who participated in the peer-led programme. The peer-led project was also considerably cheaper to implement. Similarly, a randomised controlled trial by Blondell and colleagues (2011) comparing 12-step faciliation by peer counsellors and physician-led Motivation Enhancement Therapy (MET), showed no difference in drinking-related outcomes, but a higher likelihood in the MET group of pursuing subsequent inpatient treatment. There are clear economic motives for supporting a peer-based model (inevitably peers are cheaper than professionals, particularly if they are volunteers to the role), but this is not where the benefit ends. There is a clear transition to both community ownership, empowerment of individuals and groups of peers in recovery, and offers a clear mechanism for the social contagion of recovery from one person further into their recovery journey to a person at an earlier stage.

The research evidence is supplemented by a philosophical change around the role of community and peer-based organisations in the UK to one of increased prominence, within a public health model that emphasises non-medical aspects of well-being and that promotes a change model based in the community and prioritising peer and environmental factors as enablers of lasting recovery.

Overview

There are a variety of other key influences on the recovery movement in addictions – including the desistance movement in crime and criminology, the positive psychology movement, and the user involvement and empowerment movement in both AOD and mental health – these are considered in the section on future directions in Chapter 10. However, the four overlapping areas outlined above have been especially influential in shaping the AOD recovery movement in the UK, and increasingly this is also the case in Australia. It is a movement that is still in its infancy and there is no guarantee that its evolution will be consistent across the countries that make up the UK. The early signs are that it will look very different in England than in Scotland, and inevitably there will be contextual and cultural effects on recovery growth in countries and in regions within countries. This will also be influenced by the nodes and clusters of the 'social contagion of recovery' (Christakis & Fowler, 2010), in that recovery growth will be influenced and shaped by the dominant recovery models (both the size and social acceptability of each mutual aid group and of the therapeutic communities, and by the influence of key visible recovery champions).

However, in both places there is a context of hope and a sense of revolution and change among professionals and service users that can be uncomfortable and threatening as well as exciting and exhilarating. This is the current context in which the recovery journeys outlined in proceeding chapters should be considered. The next chapter will go on to describe the context of a developmental model of addiction recovery from a personal perspective, although it is critical to bear in mind that this personal journey occurs in a context of relationships and families, networks, and the wider community. This wider community also includes professionals and services who may play a significant role in igniting or dispelling hope and belief that recovery is possible.

References

Barbic S, Krupa T & Armstrong L (2009) A randomised controlled trial of the effectiveness of a modified recovery workbook program: preliminary findings. *Psychiatric Services* **60** (4) 491–497.

Best D (2012) *Addiction Recovery: A movement for personal change and social growth in the UK.* Brighton: Pavilion.

Betty Ford Institute Consensus Panel (2007) What is recovery? A working definition from the Betty Ford Institute. *Journal of Substance Abuse Treatment* **33** 221–228.

Blondell RD, Frydrych LM, Jaanimagi U, Ashrafioun L, Homish GG, Foschio EM *et al* (2011) A randomized trail of two behavioral interventions to improve outcomes following inpatient detoxification for alcohol dependence. *Journal of Addictive Disorders* **30** (2) 136–148.

Christakis N & Fowler J (2010) *Connected: The amazing power of social networks and how they shape our lives.* Harper Press: London.

Deegan P (1993) Recovering our sense of value after being labelled mentally ill. *Journal of Psychosocial Nursing and Mental Health* **31** 7–11.

Deegan P (1998) Recovery: the lived experience of rehabilitation. *Psychosocial Rehabilitation Journal* **11** 11–19.

DeLeon G (2000) *The Therapeutic Community: Theory, model and method.* Springer Publishing Inc: New York, NY.

Donovan D M & Floyd AS (2008) Facilitating Involvement in Twelve-Step Programs. In: GM & KLA (Eds) *Recent Developments in Alcoholism* (Vol. 18, p303–320). New York: Springer.

Fukui D, Davidson L & Rapp C (2010) Pathways to recovery: a peer-led group intervention. *Psychiatric Services* **61** 944.

Galanter M, Castameda R & Salamon I (1987) Institutional self-help therapy for alcoholism: clinical outcome. *Alcoholism: Clinical and Experimental Research* **11** (5) 424–429.

Gossop M, Marsden J, Stewart D & Kidd T (2003) The National Treatment Outcome Research Study (NTORS): 4-5 year follow-up results. *Addiction* **98** 291–303.

Harding C, Brooks G, Ashikage T, Strauss J & Brier A (1987) The Vermont longitudinal study of persons with severe mental illness II: long-term outcomes of subjects who retrospectively met DSM-III criteria for schizophrenia. *American Journal of Psychiatry* **144** 727–735.

Hibbert L & Best D (2011) Assessing recovery and functioning in former problem drinkers at different stages of their recovery journey. *Drug and Alcohol Review* **30** 12–20.

HM Government (2010) *Drug Strategy 2010: Reducing demand, restricting supply, building recovery: Supporting people to live a drug-free life*. London: HO.

Humphreys K (2004) *Circles of Recovery: Self-help organizations for addictions*. Cambridge: Cambridge University Press.

Humphreys K & Lembke A (2013) Recovery-oriented policy and care systems in the United Kingdom and United States. *Drug and Alcohol Review* DOI: 10.1111/dar.12092.

Kelly JF & Yeterian JD (2008) Mutual-help groups. In W O'Donohue & JR Cunningham (Eds.) *Evidence-Based Adjunctive Treatments*. (pp. 61–105) New York: Elsevier.

Kelly JF & White W (2011) *Addiction Recovery Management: Theory, research and practice*. Humana Press: New York.

Leamy M, Bird V, Le Boutillier C, Williams J & Slade M (2011) Conceptual framework for personal recovery in mental health: systematic review and narrative synthesis. *British Journal of Psychiatry* **199** 445–452.

Litt M, Kadden R, Kabela-Cormier E & Petry N (2007a) Changing network support for drinking: Initial findings from the network support project. *Journal of Consulting and Clinical Psychology* **75** 542–555.

Litt M, Kadden R, Kabela-Cormier E *et al* (2007b) Changing network support as a prognostic indicator of drinking outcomes: the COMBINE study. *Journal of Studies of Alcohol and Drugs* **71** 837–846.

Lopez-Gaston R, Best D, Day E & White W (2010) Perceptions of 12-step interventions among UK substance misuse patients attending residential in-patient treatment in a UK treatment setting. *Journal of Groups in Addiction and Recovery* **5** 306–323.

Malivert M, Matseas M & Denis C (2012) Effectiveness of therapeutic communities: a systematic review. *European Addiction Research* **18** 1–11.

McCartney D (2012) Mutual aid groups in the UK, personal communication.

Obama B (2010) Presidential Proclamation for National Alcohol and Drug Addiction Recovery Month.

Repper J & Perkins R (2003) *Social Inclusion and Recovery: A model for mental health practice*. London: Balliere Tindall.

Scottish Government (2008) *The Road to Recovery*. Edinburgh: Scottish Government.

Sheedy CK & Whitter M (2009) *Guiding Principles and Elements of Recovery-Oriented Systems of Care: What Do We Know From the Research?* HHS Publication No. (SMA) 09-4439. Rockville, MD: Center for Substance Abuse Treatment, Substance Abuse and Mental Health Services Administration.

Slade M (2009) *Personal Recovery and Mental Illness: A guide for health professionals*. Cambridge: Cambridge University Press.

Substance Abuse and Mental Health Services Administration (2014) Recovery month [online]. Available at: http://recoverymonth.gov (accessed January 2014).

Timko C, Dixon K & Moos R (2005) Treatment for dual diagnosis patients in the psychiatric and substance abuse systems. *Mental Health Services Research* **7** (4) 229–242.

UK Drug Policy Commission (2008) *The UK Drug Policy Commission Recovery Consensus Group: A vision of recovery*. London: HM Government.

Valentine P (2011) Peer-based recovery support services within a recovery community organisation: The CCAR experience. In: J Kelly & W White (Eds) *Addiction Recovery Management: Theory, research and practice*. Springer, New York: Humana Press.

Warner R (2010) Does the scientific evidence support the recovery model? *The Psychiatrist* **34** 3–5.

White WL (1998) *Slaying the Dragon: The history of addiction treatment and recovery in America*. Bloomington, Il: Chestnut Health Systems/Lighthouse Institute.

White W (2008) *Recovery Management and Recovery-Oriented Systems of Care: Scientific rationale and promising practices*. Pittsburgh, PA: Northeast Addiction Technology Transfer Center, Great Lakes Addiction Technology Transfer Center, Philadelphia Department of Behavioral Health and Mental Retardation Services.

White WL (2009a) The mobilization of community resources to support long-term addiction recovery. *Journal of Substance Abuse Treatment* **36** (2) 146–158. doi: 10.1016/j.jsat.2008.10.006

White W (2009b) *Peer-Based Addiction Recovery Support: History, theory, practice and scientific evaluation*. Chicago, IL: Great Lakes Addiction Technology Transfer Center and Philadelphia Department of Behavioral Health and Mental Retardation Services.

Chapter 2: Theoretical and developmental model of growth in recovery capital

Introduction

Although there has been relatively little research done on the area of remission from problem drug use, Calabria *et al* (2010) conducted a systematic review of prospective research studies investigating remission rates from four substances. They concluded that '*almost one quarter of persons dependent on amphetamines, one in five dependent on cocaine, 15% of those dependent on heroin and one in 10 of those dependent on cannabis may remit from active drug dependence in a given year*' (p747). Perhaps more strikingly, White (2012) reviewed overall remission rates in a review analysis of 415 scientific reports between 1868 and 2011, and concluded that an average of 49.9% of those with a lifetime substance use disorder will eventually achieve stable recovery (and this rate increases to 53.9% in studies published since the year 2000). White also argues that between 5.3–15.3% of the adult population of the US are in recovery from a substance use disorder. This would suggest that in the US alone there are more than 25 million people in recovery (not including those in recovery from tobacco problems). This has two incredibly powerful implications – the first that there is a global army of millions in recovery (with potentially one in 10 in all large population centres in the western world) and that overcoming recovery is a common experience in the long term.

The current chapter aims to identify the processes that are associated with changes in substance use and how that relates to other key aspects of recovery, and why this should be considered as a developmental process of social identity change.

There are a relatively small number of long-term outcome studies that have been carried out in the addictions field that provide sufficient continuity and duration to map 'career' or life course changes in substance use and related behaviours. Vaillant (2003) conducted the best-known of the long-term studies, a 60-year outcome study of alcoholic men, reporting that around two-thirds of the formerly alcoholic men who were still alive by the age of 70 were abstinent and only around one-quarter were still using alcohol. In this sample, AA attendance was strongly associated with relapse prevention while the other strong predictive factors for recovery were finding a non-pharmacological substitute for alcohol, new relationships and involvement in spiritual programmes. This is entirely consistent with a recovery model based on the development of a new identity that brings with it new activities, roles and norms for behaviour.

In a second US study, on this occasion following 1,326 substance dependent males recruited from public addiction services in Chicago between 1996 and 1998, Dennis *et al* (2005) reported that the median duration of addiction careers was 27 years and the median treatment career was around nine years (covering 3–4 episodes of treatment) before one year of abstinence was achieved. This study supports the notion of long-term change, but also provides a cautionary note in two respects – first, that there is huge variation in the duration of an addiction career and second, that recovery is not a linear process and that a number of attempts (with or without formal treatment) may be required.

In another key outcome study from the US, from California, Hser *et al* (2007) reported that 43% of 242 individuals followed up after 33 years had been stably abstinent from heroin for five years or more, but Hser *et al* (2007) pointed out that most of those who achieve long-term recovery have ceased their active use in the first 10 years of their addiction career. Using the same kind of life course methodology, Grella and Lovinger (2011) interviewed 343 members of the surviving cohort of an earlier study 30 years after initial recruitment. The population were heroin addicts enrolled in a Californian methadone maintenance programme. The findings suggested four distinct groups:

1. About 25% of the sample made a relatively rapid decrease in heroin use and quit about 10–20 years after initiation.
2. 15% made a more moderate decrease before quitting after 10–20 years.
3. 25% gradually decreased their heroin use over the 30 year follow-up window.
4. 25% did not reduce their heroin use at all, and were still using at the 30-year follow-up.

This is a useful model of trajectories of change that is consistent with the work done by Hser *et al* (2007) on developmental pathways.

More recently, as cited above, White (2012) reviewed 415 scientific studies of recovery outcomes (79 community studies, 276 adult clinical studies, and 60 adolescent clinical studies) and found that of adults surveyed in the general population who once met lifetime criteria for substance use disorders, an average of 49.9% (53.9% in studies conducted since 2000) no longer met those criteria at the time of the survey. In community studies reporting both remission rates and abstinence rates for substance use disorders, an average of 43.5% of people who have ever had these disorders achieved remission, but only 17.9% did so through a strategy of complete abstinence (White, 2012). So the evidence is increasingly suggesting that people do recover, but that in the community, and probably among the less problematic and dependent, that recovery may not necessitate complete abstinence from all substances.

One conclusion that can be drawn from these studies is that many people do achieve long-term recovery from substance problems including substance dependence but that it is a complex process that can take many years and with no guarantee of long-term success. Relapse risks may diminish in the years following abstinence-oriented treatment but they never drop to zero, and there is an ongoing risk. The evidence from Dennis *et al* (2005) also suggests that change does not occur in a straightforward or linear fashion and individuals may require a number of attempts before sustained recovery is achieved. The underlying notion of the developmental pathways that link to recovery is explored in the next section.

Developmental pathways and turning points

Hser *et al* (2007) identified that key concepts in life course or developmental research include trajectories, transitions, and turning points. Trajectories refer to a line of development during a person's life, such as parenthood, work–life, drug use or offending behaviour. Trajectories are long-term patterns of behaviour, and they are marked by 'transitions'. Transitions are distinct events, like starting or finishing school or employment, or a first crime or first drug use. Although transitions are marked occasions, their consequences might be longer. Elder (1985) pointed out that the ways in which people adapt to events in their lives, and to transitions, is of major importance, as differences will result in different trajectories. This is one of the assumptions that underpins the idea of resilience – that some individuals have the strengths and resources to cope with and overcome adverse events. The third concept – a turning point – is a change in the long-term pathway (or life trajectory), which was initiated at an earlier point in time (Elder, 1985).

Turning points happen when transitions and trajectories interlock. Turning points may create positive or negative outcomes, and may be concerned with events over which a person has some, little, or no control or choice. Sometimes turning points are abrupt and radical experiences, while for others (Teruya & Hser (2010) argue for most), turning points occur over time, as a process, and are more gradual and subtle in nature. Life events in the course of people's lives have the potential to shut down or open up opportunities in the future (Teruya & Hser, 2010), and will have positive or negative consequences for the individual. While recovery initiation is a positive turning point, it is not a protector against adverse life events. However, the concept of recovery capital outlined below is about the accrual of resources that will allow individuals to cope with adverse events (resilience) or to maximise the opportunities afforded by positive turning points.

The life course model is one that has been developed by Hser *et al* (2007) as a mechanism for understanding the long-term developmental pathways that apply in all our lives – the crucial impact of major life events such as new relationships and job opportunities, the impact of moving home to a new area, and the traumatic consequences of death of loved ones and other significant forms of loss, such as divorce or sudden unemployment. There is no clear definition of what constitutes a 'major' life event and the impact of an event will differ across individuals and groups, and some events will grow in significance with the passage of time. Furthermore, events have significance in their own right but also as triggers for new trajectories. Thus, some 'major' life events will establish new trajectories that will shift the likelihood of other events occurring or arising.

One of the key consequences of a major event is that it is likely to change the environmental characteristics that the individual experiences. For instance, a person starting a new relationship and spending much of their free time in the exclusive company of their new partner will be exposed less often to the risks and opportunities experienced by their wider social networks they will, in all probability, regard such opportunities or risks with lower salience as the new relationship has changed their attitudes and values as much as it changes their repertoire of behaviours. This is crucial to our understanding of the nature of developmental recovery. Chapter 7 will use a developmental life course perspective as a frame for understanding the recovery journeys and pathways of addiction professionals who have overcome their own adverse life events.

In the Glasgow Recovery Study (Best *et al*, 2012) there were two key factors that predicted better quality of life in recovery, that were independent of the duration of recovery. The first of these was activity (parenting, group membership, volunteering, training and education, and employment) and the second was the amount of time spent with other people in recovery. However, these factors were seen as dynamic, in that the emergence of positive and recovery-oriented social networks was seen as supporting and enabling the accessibility of activity, and this in turn led to expansions of the social network. Additional qualitative analysis of this study is presented in Chapter 4, but for the rationale for the book, the key concept is both to understand the turning points that enabled individuals to initiate recovery journeys but also those that supported the subsequent positive recovery trajectory. In the developmental social identity model, the assumption is that the recovery trajectory is nurtured through positive social role models and recovery group participation, with Rudolph Moos having provided a framework for this change based on his work with long-term recovery among alcoholics. This model was laid out by Moos in terms of psychological mechanisms that are inherent to the recovery process (Moos, 2007):

(i) Social control theory

This involves strong bonds to family, friends, work, religion and other aspects of traditional society that motivate individuals to refrain from substance use. Tonigan and Rice (2010) reported a fourfold reduction in relapse rates among AA members who had a sponsor compared to those that did not. Social control is best understood as the rules of group membership in that it is the informal norms, roles and rules that underpin group activity and that are fundamental to the membership of the group. Thus, if one is a member of Greenpeace, it is both a tacit and overt rule that going on a whaling expedition is not acceptable. Thus, while paying a subscription and wearing the insignia are markers of membership, abiding by the values and expectations of the group are a key part of active membership.

(ii) Social learning theory

This is based on the idea that substance-specific attitudes and behaviours are learned from role models. In a trial assessing the impact of 'network support', when compared to standard case management approaches, Litt *et al* (2007) found that the addition of one clean and sober individual to the social network reduced relapse rates in drinkers by 27% in the following year. This study involved linkage to AA groups and found that clean and sober peers were an essential predictor of ongoing abstinence. The key assumption is that individuals 'learn' recovery by observing the behaviour of others that they perceive to be both attractive and successful, and that they then imitate these actions as part of developing their own recovery repertoire.

(iii) Behavioural economics theory

Desistance from substance use is linked to alternative rewards – through volunteering, educational work, other relationships, etc. Best *et al* (2012) reported that greater engagement in meaningful activities, along with more time spent with recovering peers, were associated with a higher quality of life. However, this is a conscious process based on rational decision making in which the attractiveness of recovery is perceived to exceed the temptations of relapse.

(iv) Stress and coping theory

This is based on the idea that stressful life events lead to distress and alienation and so to substance use, and that substance use is a form of avoidant coping. In a 16-year follow-up study, longer participation in AA in the first year after initial help-seeking was associated with greater levels of self-efficacy to reduce drinking at each follow-up point (Moos & Moos, 2006). Likewise, in a separate outcome study of AA, greater engagement with AA in the month after treatment completion was associated with higher levels of self-efficacy, greater commitment to abstinence, and better cognitive and behavioural coping (Morgenstern *et al,* 1996). The key to stress and coping approaches are that in recovery the individual develops the personal skills and resources to support them on their recovery journey. This will include improvements in self-esteem, self-efficacy and the basic resilience skills required to withstand the adversities and major setbacks of day-to-day life.

What the Litt study illustrates, as the Glasgow Recovery Study did, is that peers are important, in part because they shape what is seen to be possible. Changes in social networks are accompanied by changes in what is seen as attractive and desirable (characterised by Moos as behavioural economics) through a process of engagement and imitation. Part of the reason why having sober people in the social network changes relapse risk is that the individual is more likely to be among people and in places that support and promote sobriety, but that by doing so, their own evaluation of the attractiveness of sobriety also shifts and the resulting costs and disadvantages associated with drinking become evident. What carries the rather sinister label of 'social control' in the Moos model is in fact the very gradual influence of others on what is a reasonable way to behave, and how the world appears.

The other key implication of the Litt study is that it shows the importance of 'assertive linkage' to recovery groups (Timko, DeBenedetti & Billow, 2006;

Manning *et al,* 2012), meaning the generation of active processes to encourage and support engagement. The assumption is that people early in recovery may lack the self-esteem and assertiveness to engage in group activities and that they will need a push in the right direction. In the Manning *et al* (2012) study, a randomised clinical trial, this involved provision of leaflets, doctor encouragement or peer support to encourage inpatients to attend at least one mutual aid group meeting during their treatment. As would be suggested by the Humphreys and Lembke (2013) summary, the peer condition was the most successful, and it was most successful because it provided the personal direction, encouragement and role modelling necessary to initiate engagement and then to support ongoing participation.

For people to engage in group activity it will often take considerable initial encouragement and support, and assertive linkage is the sum of the strategies available to enable active engagement in groups and activities. The next section will focus not on the groups that can promote recovery but on the individuals who may or may not be members of recovery groups.

Agents of change and the role of recovery champions

In the 2010 UK Drug Strategy (HM Government, 2010), the concept of 'recovery champions' was introduced, as both agents of change within specialist treatment services and in the wider community, referred to respectively as 'therapeutic' and 'community' champions. There is also a third set of recovery champions identified in the strategy – 'strategic champions' whose role is to influence policy and create a strategic vision for recovery. In Valentine's work in Connecticut (Valentine, 2011), the 'strategic' role is around identifying and enabling the structural and systemic changes that enable recovery to influence professional processes and practices.

The relevance of the recovery champion in this space is that they act as agents of change by creating both social and contextual recovery capital – while there are people who do recover on their own (Granfield & Cloud, 2001), this is relatively unusual, and appears to occur most commonly among people with strong existing levels of personal and social resources. Granfield and Cloud (2001) reported that the respondents in their study discounted the use of self-help groups because they saw themselves as 'efficacious people' who often prided themselves on their past accomplishments. They noted that the subjects in their study *'had jobs, supportive families, high school and college credentials, and other social supports that gave them reasons to alter their drug-taking behavior,'* and add that *'having much to lose'* gave their respondents *'incentives to transform their lives'* (Granfield & Cloud, 2001, p55).

The concept of recovery champions was manipulated in a study by Best *et al* (2013) in the Yorkshire town of Barnsley. Following initial professional and peer training sessions in the community, participants were asked to self-nominate as recovery champions and to come together to form a Barnsley Recovery Coalition. This group went on to establish a range of recovery activities including a float in the Lord Mayor's Parade, a recovery walk, a family sports day and an art walk through the town. The principle of recovery champions is that they are visible beacons of hope whose active promotion of recovery activities and celebrations of recovery generate both hope and a social contagion of recovery change. In a more recent study, Best *et al* (in press) have undertaken a similar process in the town of York and have shown that the emergence of a recovery community is driven by the endeavours of a core cluster of individuals who not only link individuals, they also promote the linkages between recovery groups and communities.

For the majority of people who do not have a personal reserve of recovery resources, the catalysts may well involve key events that open the doors to new life vistas, but these openings will often be linked to people who can support or help that pathway. In the Litt *et al* (2007) study cited earlier, maintaining abstinence after detoxification is associated with having at least one sober person in the individual's social network. More explicitly, Moos (2007) talks of the importance of both social control and social learning. What does this mean? The impact of a changing social network is that it alters not only what is acceptable to those you care about and value (informal social control) it also provides you with a mechanism for learning and imitating how they successfully live the way they do. Thus, in the Litt study, the newly detoxed drinker not only spends time with someone who does not go to the pub, they are also spending time with someone who teaches them ways of coping with not drinking and who brings a value system and a set of beliefs where alternative activities are more highly valued and more highly rewarded.

This model is at the heart of the question asked in this book. As people move towards stable recovery, how and why do they change their social networks, and what difference does this make to their identity and self-perceptions? Within a life-course model, one of the key questions is: what are the events that cause change for people, but also what determines the extent of their impact in creating a new trajectory? There is then another question that will be picked up in Chapter 10 about the extent to which interventions (at the individual level as indicated in the Litt study, and at the group level as in Best studies in York and Barnsley) can be driven to increase recovery capital and so initiate and sustain recovery pathways and trigger the growth of recovery capital, a concept explored in more depth in the next section.

Recovery capital

The hypothesis that was advanced in *Addiction Recovery* (Best, 2012) was that key life events create windows of opportunity for change and that the type of change ('trajectory' in the developmental life course model) is determined by the resources and supports available to the individual at the time. This is the concept of recovery capital and this idea will be reviewed in brief below.

In its original iteration in the alcohol and other drugs field, Granfield and Cloud (2001) defined recovery capital as *'the breadth and depth of internal and external resources that can be drawn upon to initiate and sustain recovery from AOD [alcohol and other drug] problems'*. Granfield and Cloud have argued that people who have access to greater reserves of recovery capital are better able to address problems than those who do not have such access. The concept relies heavily on the idea of social capital advanced by Putnam (2000) as the *'connections among individuals – social networks and the norms of reciprocity and trustworthiness that arise from them .... Social capital can [thus] be simultaneously a 'private good' and a 'public good'. Some of the benefits from an investment in social capital goes to bystanders, while some of the benefit rebounds to the immediate interest of the person making the investment'* (p19–20). The key component of social capital is that it is reciprocal and developmental and that it is shared between people and grows with trust and support – it is more like a social contract than a bank account. People cannot simply 'draw' on social capital, rather it is an active, dynamic component of engaging with others and includes the principal's commitment to their networks, as much as the resources and goodwill that the network can offer to the principal.

In 2010, Best and Laudet introduced the concept of collective recovery capital to attempt to account for environmental variables that will influence the likelihood both that windows of opportunities arise and that the person is in a position to take advantage of them. This discussion paper considered three key environmental influences:

1. The quality of local specialist AOD treatment services, in particular their capacity to enable individuals to address acute problems (withdrawals, cravings, risk taking, and so on) and to link people into the local recovery communities and networks.

2.   The quality and availability of local recovery groups and champions, based on the idea that recovery is only achievable and sustainable with the appropriate links and supports to visible and attractive champions and groups.

3.   Finally, there are wider socio-cultural prerequisites which coalesce into a sense of community hope but are predicated on the availability of houses and jobs. This is important in convincing people that undertaking a recovery journey is worthwhile. If professionals and peers feel that recovery cannot go anywhere because there are no opportunities then it is unlikely that the initial efforts will be sustained or successful.

The rationale behind this model is that there is a complex interaction and dynamic shift across the three levels such that the social support for recovery may well be predicated on availability and access to attractive and available recovery champions and the sense of self-esteem and self-efficacy may be linked to the hope that results from realistic aspirations for stable housing and meaningful employment. This is similar to the communitarian or ecological model of social capital advanced by Whitley and McKenzie (2005), in which social capital is defined as consisting of five components:

1.   Community networks: number and density of voluntary, state and personal networks.

2.   Civic engagement and participation in civic networks.

3.   Local community identity: sense of belonging and equality with other members of the community.

4.   Norms of co-operation: a sense of obligation to others and the belief that helping others will be returned in times of need.

5.   Trust in the community.

As in the collective recovery capital model above, the basic concept is that personal resources and supports are embedded within social support systems, which are themselves located within cultural and community systems that promote or diminish the likelihood of recovery. This notion of interacting circles of support is crucial where the individual is located within a household or family, which is located within a community that is located within a culture that entails economic, legal and historical parameters. While each of these factors will influence the person's social identity as discussed below, they will also shape the resources and supports available.

An interesting analysis of this, in the context of social capital is outlined in the work of Cheong *et al* (2013) who explored asthma patients' perceptions of a range of healthcare professionals in what the authors described as their 'health networks', typically consisting of one healthcare professional and one layperson, typically a family member or friend, and it was typically family or friends who asthma sufferers turned to first, and who monitored symptoms, shared experiences and provided lifestyle advice. However, this offers an extended model of recovery capital in which professionals can constitute a key resource as part of the wider community or collective capital, irrespective of the treatments they provide, and professionals can count as part of the community capital available to support recovery.

In writing about youth culture, where the core concept is the idea of 'resilience', Runyan *et al* (1998) explored social capital as a protective factor in young children at risk of maltreatment. They found that the presence of any of four social capital factors – two parent figures in the home; support from the maternal caregiver; neighbourhood support and regular church attendance – increased the odds of children doing well by 29% (Runyan *et al,* 1998). If two factors were present, the odds of children doing well increased by 66% (Runyan *et al,* 1998). This is consistent with the notion of recovery capital, not only as a conceptual framework, but also as a metric, and this idea of recovery as something that can be benchmarked and mapped both over time and against others is an important development in the growing understanding of recovery as a process.

In our own work, we have developed the 'Assessment of Recovery Capital' Scale (Groshkova *et al,* 2012) to further this approach to measuring and mapping recovery capital in a 50-item scale of recovery assets, split between social capital and personal capital components of a wider recovery capital. This is an attempt to provide a metric that can be used to assess progress in recovery both within and beyond acute addiction treatment and to allow individuals to identify those areas that remain weaknesses in their ongoing recovery journey. This scale is used with the addiction professionals in the study and is discussed in detail in Chapter 8.

Social identity, recovery and belonging

Belonging matters to all of us. Holt-Lunstad *et al* (2010) conducted a meta-analysis of well-being studies and reported on the importance of being connected to others for both physical and psychological health. In this analysis, the acquisition of a new friend conferred the same benefit as stopping smoking in terms of the prevention of mortality, showing the importance of social connectedness to well-being. Jetten *et al* (2009) have argued that this effect is at least in part a consequence of the benefits of belonging and the identity that belonging to a group can confer. Jetten *et al* (2009) argue that, in times of stress, group membership can confer a significant benefit by enhancing the extent to which individuals receive and benefit from social support. This is the foundation for a social identity model of identity change in which identity is understood to have an intrinsically social component.

Haslam *et al* (2008), in one of a number of studies testing the empirical foundations for the social identity model, found that stroke victims who had belonged to more social groups before their stroke reported greater well-being and life satisfaction after the stroke, particularly among those who maintained those contacts after the stroke. Similarly, Iyer *et al* (2009) reported on students leaving home to go to university and found that having multiple social identities before university predicted students' adjustment and well-being once at university. However, Jetten *et al* (2009) caution that it is not simply a question of the number of identities but of their compatibility and continuity. Jetten also cautions that not all group memberships are positive and that being a member of a socially ostracised and excluded group may have adverse consequences for well-being through sustaining a negative social identity.

One of the major challenges this provokes in studying recovery from addiction is the notion of changing identities and moving to a new identity of 'recovery' – one that is not compatible with the lifestyle of self-categorisation of active addiction. The evidence from Longabaugh *et al* (2010) would suggest that it is the transition from a network supportive of drinking to a network supportive of recovery that is predictive of positive long-term recovery outcomes. But this is difficult to achieve for precisely the reasons laid out by Jetten *et al* (2009) – that there is neither compatibility nor continuity of social identities and so the experience of stress is likely to be significantly increased in this period. The transition to a new social identity of recovery will involve moving away from the incompatible using identity and this is likely to have to occur for individuals whose stigmatised status means they do not have access to multiple alternative supports and identities. It is in this context that the twin recovery beacons of 12-step and therapeutic communities offer the most accessible supports for a transition to a social identity of recovery.

This social identity transition is likely to be particularly important for substance users whose use may be sustained and their attempts to change foiled by the norms and practices of a using social network. In the COMBINE study, Longabaugh *et al* (2010) used the Important People and Activities (IPA) scale and found that frequency of social network drinking and opposition to drinking were both uniquely related to drinking days at follow-up. In other words, drinkers whose social networks support drinking typically have poorer outcomes than drinkers whose social networks support abstinence and recovery efforts. In an experimental manipulation of this effect, Litt *et al* (2007) reported that assigning detoxified drinkers to a 'network support' condition that added at least one sober person to the participant's social network had a marked effect on their likelihood to relapse – their chances of relapsing in the first year after detox reduced by 27%.

The social identity model offers an explanatory framework for the transition from use to recovery as a socially mediated process involving the development of a new (not 'restored') identity that emerges through engagement in recovery groups and time spent with recovery champions. In their book *The Social Cure* (2011), Jetten *et al* offer a model, which suggests that identity is both individual and social, and that the adoption of responses in particular contexts is shaped in part by the salience of available social identities. Thus, if through exposure to recovery in a therapeutic community or by repeated involvement in mutual aid groups, the social identity of recovery is available, attractive and has been proven to be functional and beneficial in the past, then it is likely that this is the identity that will be dominant in the response to risk situations, and so recovery may be sustained. This model offers a framework for recovery both in terms of how it is initially transmitted from one person to another and, secondly, how it is sustained that will be explored in more depth as this book progresses.

A developmental model of recovery capital

Best (2012) outlines a model of recovery capital that is based on the developmental trajectory model outlined by Hser *et al* (2007) linked to the idea of recovery capital as the source of 'currency' for change. In this model, the basic developmental approach is adopted in which lives have trajectories whose course is influenced by significant life events and life transitions. The current work attempts to assess and test part of this model by examining the life stories of people in recovery to assess the impact of major life events and how this is understood in terms of developmental pathways and recovery resources. In other words, people's lives continue in particular directions on fairly stable pathways, until big events happen that can send the person spiralling off in a completely different direction. This can be good or bad (a new relationship or job, a death of a loved one) and can be planned or unexpected, but it is a continuing process that happens to all of us.

Writing on the new subject of 'positive criminology', Ronel and Elisha (2011) use the concept of criminal spin to describe an escalating criminal career of risk taking and increasing frequency and seriousness of offending. However, they also discuss the reverse process for desistance from offending where key events such as exposure to self-help groups, social acceptance and positive life changes can act as significant catalysts for a virtuous circle of life improvement. This is entirely consistent with the idea of a trajectory that gathers momentum based on the emergence of new contexts that shape both the resources available to the individual (recovery capital) and the identities through which these contexts are viewed and framed. The notion of social identity is crucial here as it provides not only a sense of belonging and well-being that arises from being a member of a valued group, but also shapes the attitudes, norms, beliefs and values of the members of the group. In other words, being a member of a therapeutic community not only confers a sense of safety and belonging, it also inculcates the beliefs and values of the TC for as long as that identity remains salient to the individual, and will have a residual effect depending on what the person does next.

Thus, the likelihood of recovery is shaped by life trajectories and events that would have the potential to be negative or positive. Drug or alcohol treatment is designed to increase recovery capital by addressing acute needs (physical and mental health) and by providing direct interventions and links to other services that can help to develop the skills and resources needed for the longer term recovery pathways and journeys. However, not all treatment episodes are successful – the client may not respond well to the treatment offered, the therapeutic relationship may fail to develop (and so the social capital of a health network does not grow), or in the cases of residential treatment, withdrawals may be too severe and the client can drop out and relapse early on. In all of these cases, the person may end up with a sense of failure, of hopelessness and feeling that they are worse off than when they entered the new treatment episode – and so treatment may result in a net reduction in recovery capital. In other words, the tipping point may be negative, and may result in a loss of personal capital in the form of diminished self-esteem and self-efficacy. And no matter how good the treatment is, the person may be thrown back into the same social network and physical environment and so be subject to the same pressures and contingencies. In other words, what looked like a tipping point may have been little more than a blip in an ongoing addiction career. This is part of the reason why 'stable' recovery is typically estimated to take around five years to achieve (White, 2009).

In contrast, for clients who enter a treatment service that leads to improved physical and mental well-being, that gives them a sense of purpose and a sense of hope, and that provides positive social networks and role models, the trajectory is likely to be positive, and allow a significant change in both personal capital (a sense of achievement and hope that generates self-esteem and positive coping skills) and social capital in the form of friends that support recovery and who role model successful recovery approaches and techniques (White, 2009; Moos, 2007). But why would some clients fail and others succeed in treatment, and even more perplexingly, why would some clients fail a number of times in treatment before finally succeeding and achieving lasting recovery? The answer is partly that offered by Zinberg (1984) in relation to variable substance effects – that the person is not actually the same on each occasion! While the individual experience may differ while receiving the treatment, the key point about the developmental model of recovery capital is that the person will most likely be in a different place, arriving with a different bundle of strengths and resources, aspirations and plans. It is the interaction of the individual's recovery capital with the candidate turning point that generates the trajectory change in life-course. To continue the treatment analogy, if the person completes an inpatient detoxification motivated by belief that they can recover, hope for the future, strong coping wand relapse prevention skills and has people to rely on and things to do on departure, their chances of sustaining the positive trajectory are significantly enhanced. But this initial gain in well-being needs to be nurtured and sustained and that is why the three core concepts – a positive social identity of recovery, growing recovery capital and a positive developmental recovery trajectory – are seen as critical to the recovery journey.

The concept of recovery capital is still at a very early stage of operationalisation – the development of the Assessment of Recovery Capital (ARC; Groshkova *et al,* 2012) is not the first attempt to create a recovery capital measurement tool, but these have had relatively little impact so far on research or clinical practice. However, the assumption of the ARC (and other recovery instruments) is that recovery capital is quantifiable, and that there are underlying clusters of recovery resources – primarily social and personal recovery factors. While this is complicated by the potential impact of community resources (Best & Laudet, 2010), it would suggest that there is the possibility of developing a yardstick for mapping and measuring basic recovery resources at different phases of the recovery journey. It also links with the idea of social identity theory in which the recovery identity is internalised following exposure to attractive recovery role models and is nurtured through engagement in recovery supports and activities.

It is crucial to emphasise that this model places the social at the centre of the change process. This is a model in which other people matter – they can be the catalyst and the inspiration for change and they can be the social models and mentors that support it. Critically, the role other people will play will be around supporting and sustaining change – it is within a life-course model that the social world has a prime role in maintaining gains made, in creating the sense of belonging and positive social identity and the belief systems that recovery is possible and life meaningful without alcohol or drugs. The social world is also the prism through which the recovery identity emerges and is sustained as it becomes the salient social identity for managing challenging life events.

In the current book, the main study that will explore this model involves a group of addiction professionals in long-term recovery who were asked to take part in an in-depth recovery research project to assess their recovery experiences and recovery journeys. This process consists of detailed history taking before assessing their own narratives of the recovery journey. Before these detailed stories are relayed and their messages outlined, Chapter 3 will provide an overview of the stories collected from a much more disparate group of people in recovery in Glasgow, collected as part of the Glasgow Recovery Study (described in Best *et al*, 2011), while Chapter 4 will look at an Australian sample of online recovery stories that relate to the developmental components of turning points and trajectories.

References

Best D, Gow J, Taylor A, Knox T & White W (2011) Reccovery from heroin or alcohol dependence: a qualitative account of the recovery experience in Glasgow. *Journal of Drug Issues* **11** (1) 359–378.

Best D (2012) *Addiction Recovery: A movement for personal change and social growth in the UK.* Brighton: Pavilion.

Best D, Gow J, Taylor A, Groshkova T & White W (2012) Mapping the recovery stories of drinkers and drug users in Glasgow: quality of life and its associations with measures of recovery capital. *Drug and Alcohol Review* **31** (3) 334–341.

Best D & Laudet A (2010) *The Potential for Recovery Capital.* Royal Society for the Arts. RSA: London.

Best D, Loudon L, Powell D, Groshkova T & White W (2013) Identifying and recruiting recovery champions: exploratory action research in Barnsley, South Yorkshire. *Journal of Groups in Addiction and Recovery* **8** (3) 169–184.

Best D, McKitterick T, Beswick T & Savic M (in press) Recovery capital and social networks among people in treatment and among those in recovery in York, England. *Alcoholism Treatment Quarterly* (in press).

Calabria B, Degenhardt L, Briegleb C, Vos T, Hall W, Lynskey M, Callaghan B, Rana U & McLaren J (2010) Systematic review of prospective studies investigating "remission" from amphetamine, cannabis, cocaine or opioid dependence. *Addictive Behaviours* **35** 741–749.

Cheong L, Armour C & Bosnich-Anticevich S (2013) Primary health care teams and the patient perspective: a social network analysis. *Research in Social and Administrative Pharmacy* **9** 741–757.

Dennis M, Scott C, Funk R & Foss M (2005) The duration and correlates of addiction and treatment careers. *Journal of Substance Abuse Treatment* **28** 851–862.

Elder GH (1985) Perspectives on the life course. In: GH Elder (Ed) *Life Course Dynamics*. Ithaca, NY: Cornell University Press.

Granfield R & Cloud W (2001) Social context and 'natural recovery': the role of social capital in the resolution of drug-associated problems. *Substance Use and Misuse* **36** (11) 1543–1570.

Grella C & Lovinger K (2011) 30-year trajectories of heroin and other drug use among men and women sampled from methadone treatment in California. *Drug and Alcohol Dependence* **118** 251–258.

Groshkova T, Best D & White W (2012) The Assessment of Recovery Capital: Properties and psychometrics of a measure of addiction recovery strengths. *Drug and Alcohol Review* DOI: 10.1111/j.1465-3362.2012.00489.x.

Haslam C, Holme A, Haslam SA, Iyer A, Jetten J & Williams WH (2008) Maintaining group memberships: Social identity predicts well-being after stroke. *Neuropsychological Rehabilitation* **18** 671–691.

HM Government (2010) *Drug Strategy 2010 – Reducing demand, restricting supply, building recovery: Supporting people to live a drug free life*. London: HM Government.

Holt-Lunstad J, Smith TB & Layton JB (2010) Social relationships and mortality risk: a meta-analytic review. *PLoS Medicine* **7** (7) e1000316.

Humphreys K & Lembke A (2013) Recovery-Oriented Policy and Care Systems in the United Kingdom and United States. *Drug and Alcohol Review* DOI: 10.1111/dar.12092.

Hser Y, Longshore D & Anglin M (2007) The life course perspective on drug use: a conceptual framework for understanding drug use trajectories evaluation review. *Journal of Drug Issues* **31** 515–547.

Iyer A, Jetten J, Tsivrikos D, Haslam SA & Postmes T (2009) The more (and the more compatible) the merrier: multiple group memberships and identity compatibility as predictors of adjustment after life transitions. *British Journal of Social Psychology* **48** 707–733.

Jetten J, Haslam SA, Iyer A & Haslam C (2009) Turning to others in times of change: Shared identity and coping with stress. In: S Stürmer and M Snyder (Eds) *New Directions in the Study of Helping: Group-level perspectives on motivations, consequences and interventions* (pp 139–156). Chichester: Wiley-Blackwell.

Jetten J, Haslam C & Haslam SA (Eds.) (2011) *The Social Cure: Identity, health and well-being*. New York: Psychology Press.

Litt M, Kadden R, Kabela-Cormier E & Petry N (2007) Changing network support for drinking: initial findings from the network support project. *Journal of Consulting and Clinical Psychology* **75** 542–555.

Longabaugh R, Wirtz P, Zywiak W & O'Malley S (2010) Network support as a prognostic indicator of drinking outcomes: The COMBINE study. *Journal of Studies on Alcohol and Drugs* **71** 837–846.

Manning V, Best D, Faulkner N, Titherington E, Morinan A, Keaney F, Gossop M & Strang J (2012) Does active referral by a doctor or 12-step peer improve 12-step meeting attendance? Results from a pilot randomised control trial. *Drug and Alcohol Dependence* **26** (1–2) 131–137.

Moos R (2007) Theory-based active ingredients of effective treatments for substance use disorders. *Drug and Alcohol Dependence* **88** (2–3) 109–121.

Moos RH & Moos SB (2006) Rates and predictors of relapse after natural and treated remission from alcohol use disorders. *Addiction* **101** (2) 212–222.

Morgenstern J, Kahler CW, Frey RM & Labouvie E (1996) Modeling therapeutic response to 12-step treatment: optimal responders, nonresponders, partial responders. *Journal of Substance Abuse* **8** (1) 45–59.

Putnam R (2000) *Bowling Alone: The collapse and revival of American community*. New York: Simon and Schuster.

Ronel N & Elisha E (2011) A different perspective: introducing positive criminology. *International Journal of Offender Therapy and Comparative Criminology* **55** (2) 305–325.

Runyan D, Hunter W, Socolar R, Amaya-Jackson L, English D, Landswerk J, Dubowitz H, Browne D, Bangdiwala S & Matthew R (1998) Children who prosper in unfavourable environments: the relationship to social capital. *Pediatrics* **101** (1) 3–18.

Teruya C & Hser Y-I (2010) Turning points in the life course: current findings and future directions in drug use research. *Current Drug Abuse Review* **3** (3) 189–195.

Timko C, DeBenedetti A & Billow R (2006) Intensive referral to 12-step self-help groups and 6-month substance use disorder outcomes. *Addiction* **101** (5) 678–688.

Tonigan JS & Rice SL (2010) Is it beneficial to have an Alcoholics Anonymous sponsor? *Psychology of Addictive Behaviors* **24** (3) 397–403.

Vaillant G (2003) A 60-year follow-up of alcoholic men. *Addiction* **98** 1043–1051.

Valentine P (2011) Peer based recovery support services within a recovery community organisation: The CCAR experience. In: J Kelly & W White (Eds) *Addiction Recovery Management: Theory, research and practice*. New York: Humana Springer.

White W (2009) The mobilisation of community resources to support long-term addiction recovery. *Journal of Substance Abuse Treatment* **36** (2) 146–158.

White W (2012) *Recovery / Remission From Substance Use Disorders: An analysis of reported outcomes in 415 scientific reports, 1868–2011*. Philadelphia, PA: Philadelphia Department of Behavioral Health and Intellectual Disability Services and the Great Lakes Addiction Technology Transfer Center.

Whitley R & McKenzie K (2005) Social capital and psychiatry: review of the literature. *Harvard Review of Psychiatry* **13** 71–84.

Zinberg N (1984) *Drug, Set and Setting: The basis for controlled intoxicant use*. New York: Yale University Press.

Chapter 3: Recovery stories in the Glasgow Recovery Study

This chapter outlines the previous research undertaken by the researcher in this area, which shaped the rationale and method for the Glasgow Recovery Study (Best *et al*, 2011 a, b) and describes the main quantitative findings from that study before going on to look at the qualitative findings that are relevant to the developmental and social recovery model outlined here.

Background to the study

In 2007, I was asked to lead a research study looking at successful experiences and stories, which was published the following year and became the foundation for the first recovery pathways study I had been involved in. This project involved 108 former heroin addicts who were working in the alcohol and drug fields who responded to a short questionnaire asking them about their recovery pathways and experiences. On average, they had been in recovery for just under 10 years, following a heroin using career that also lasted just under 10 years, punctuated by an average of 2.6 episodes of treatment. When participants were asked how they finally managed to stop using heroin, their reasons were 'internal' – typically that they had tired of the lifestyle and then a trigger event (a health scare, a relationship break-up, an arrest) had been the final straw. However, when they were then asked how they had managed to sustain their recovery, their answers were much more 'external' and related to other people, typically involving moving away from their peer network of fellow users and moving into social networks of non-users, typically other people in recovery (Best *et al*, 2008). This frequently involved a physical relocating, but inevitably involved a change in social networks.

The next study in this series (Hibbert & Best, 2011) was undertaken in Birmingham where we recruited former dependent drinkers who were in recovery – either between one and five years in recovery (there were 35 participants in this category) or more than five years in recovery (there were 18 participants with more than five years of recovery time). Our initial aim was to assess the quality of life of those in long-term recovery using the World Health Organization Brief Quality of Life assessment (Skevington *et al*, 2004). As hypothesised, those in recovery for longer had better quality of life – particularly in the areas of social well-being and satisfaction in their lived environment. The study also suggested that quality of life continued to grow the longer people remained in recovery.

The final study in this sequence was also undertaken in Birmingham, exploring the recovery journeys of 132 people in medicated recovery and 87 in abstinent recovery (Best *et al*, 2011a). Those in maintained recovery were more anxious about using heroin and had lower self-efficacy, worse physical health, poorer quality of life, and more peer group members still using. Being older was associated with greater quality of life (rather than time since last use) supporting a 'maturing out' hypothesis. In both the abstinent and the medicated groups, there were relationships between time since last heroin use and reduction in negative symptoms (such as anxiety and depression) and growth of positive strengths (self-esteem and quality of life). This study provides further support for a developmental model in which recovery is seen as a life-course transition in which symptoms reduce as resources and strengths emerge, and it is clear that what initially prompts a recovery journey is only partly predictive of what will sustain it.

The Glasgow Recovery Study

In 2009, I was commissioned (as part of a research team from the University of the West of Scotland) by the local provider agency, Glasgow Addiction Services (GAS) to undertake a study investigating the recovery experiences of people in Glasgow. This was designed to measure the effectiveness of the local treatment services in adequately engaging clients in recovery groups and communities. The method agreed upon was a mixed methods approach collecting both qualitative and quantitative data, so that the basic event history of each recovery journey was supplemented with more in-depth personal and experiential narrative about the person's experiences and history.

A team of students was recruited from a post-graduate diploma course in alcohol and drugs to undertake the interviews and the team worked with me to develop the interview schedule, to support its passage through the ethics committee and to pilot the instrument. There were four research students who supported my work in interviewing for the project and the team remained together for the duration of the study. As with all recovery studies, one of the major issues was in identifying and recruiting a sample, and in our study we decided on three main strategies:

1. From community and aftercare groups (including the mutual aid groups, Alcoholics Anonymous and Narcotics Anonymous).

2. Through snowballing from personal contacts and from successful interviews.

3. Through media advertising through local and free newspapers.

In the event, very few people were recruited from the media component and most were identified through aftercare services and community groups, with Alcoholics Anonymous particularly helpful in generating engagement among its members. The next main challenge was around the definition of who is appropriate for inclusion with existing studies varying markedly in the rigidity of their definitions – thus, Laudet *et al* (2006) undertook formal screening to assess formal diagnostic criteria for lifetime dependence. In this study, our aim was to be much more flexible and participant-driven in our inclusion definition, which was finalised as *'someone who believes that at some point in their lives they were dependent on alcohol or heroin, but they have not used that primary substance for the last 12 months, and they believe themselves to be either recovered or in recovery'* (Best *et al*, 2011a).

Through this process a total of 205 adults with a history of either alcohol or heroin dependence were recruited to the study (107 former drinkers and 98 former heroin users). The key findings from the quantitative component of the study were that the average time dependent for heroin users was 10.8 years and for drinkers 15.7 years, but onset and desistance were earlier for the heroin users, suggesting that recovery typically starts earlier for heroin users. Additionally, longer periods of time since last use of alcohol or heroin was associated with better quality of life, consistent with the previous work in Birmingham. Greater engagement in meaningful activities was associated with better functioning, and was associated with quality of life, followed by number of peers in recovery in the social network. Heroin users in abstinent recovery generally reported better functioning than those in maintained recovery.

So the main quantitative finding from the Glasgow Recovery Study was that well-being and functioning was associated with greater engagement in meaningful activities, and with more engagement with other people also in recovery, but that this association was to some extent mediated by time – in other words people learn to recover and to get the most out of their peer networks and their community engagement. This is fundamental to the hypothesis that recovery is a social and learned behaviour that becomes entrenched through changes in activities, social structures and socially mediated values and beliefs. There was almost no effect of spending time with people who had never been users and, more surprisingly, no adverse effect of spending time with people who were still users, but there was a clear benefit to having a social network including others in recovery. This is consistent with a literature that suggests that those who have the capacity to build social connections with people supportive of their recovery will have better outcomes (Longabaugh *et al,* 2010).

The qualitative component of the Glasgow Recovery Study

The key questions explored in the qualitative section of the interview were:

- How does the individual define recovery and what does it mean for them?
- What enabled drug and alcohol users to start on their recovery journeys?
- What was found to be helpful in early recovery, and in sustaining recovery?
- What role, if any, did treatment play in the recovery journey?
- What social and group supports were accessed during recovery?
- Where did they see themselves as being at the time of the interview?

Once the questionnaire component of the research interview was completed, the researcher confirmed that the participant was willing to continue and that they were happy for the qualitative section of the interview to be tape recorded. Data was collected between May and September 2009. Participants' responses to open questions on recovery were recorded electronically in most of the interviews, and were handwritten if a recording handset was unavailable. The sound files were transcribed. All the qualitative responses from interviews and from self-complete questionnaires were then analysed. Initial inspection of the data indicated that there were few differences between the types of data (interview transcriptions, researchers' handwritten notes, self-complete questionnaires) in the experiences reported or the views expressed. Qualitative analysis, initially question by question, identified initial themes and content that was then explored across the research team.

This work has been written up in one research paper (Best *et al,* 2011b), with the key findings from this paper suggesting that recovery was understood as including but transcending freedom from dependence, and that most participants saw their own recovery as an ongoing process rather than a time-limited milestone with a finite completion point. This is particularly the case for those who were actively involved in the 12-step movement but, irrespective of this, very few of the sample described themselves as 'recovered'. Nonetheless, the recovery journey for many people was no longer about substance use and was more likely to be about wider life changes and developments.

The journey of recovery was not generally seen to stop with successful cessation of substance use but to transcend this and involve a life transformation that was typically experienced as ongoing and, in many cases, anticipated to be lifelong. The motivating factors for starting the recovery journey were usually negative personal experiences – with former heroin users more likely to cite 'the lifestyle' and former alcohol users their behaviour and health problems – and more positively around issues of personal identity. Social factors were often cited as key in sustaining recovery, especially peer support, reflecting consistently the findings of the Best *et al* (2008) study with addiction professionals in recovery from heroin dependence. The re-analysis presented in the remainder of this chapter will re-examine this qualitative material within a social, developmental framework that is focused on the idea of trajectories and tipping points that are generated by the complex interaction of social and developmental factors. The reconciling of qualitative and quantitative data will be central to the model for change outlined in the new interviews on recovery transitions and pathways.

Developmental pathways and change

For a number of the participants there was, to borrow the language of 12-step fellowships, a sense of having hit a 'rock bottom' in which they had lost all self-respect and self-esteem. One participant described this experience as guilt –'*I just felt I was letting myself down, letting a lot of people down*', while another respondent reflected back on '*The places I had to go, and people I had to deal with, and the things I had to do to get it*'. This sense of descent is summed up in the belief that '*I couldn't go on any longer, probably the mental aspect. (…) I had to stop. It was either that or die*'. At least in retrospect, the experience of the turning point generally had the quality of a gradual and cumulative descent to the point where the individual neither knew nor liked themselves and that the recovery journey was an active attempt to arrest this decline – as outlined in the comment that: '*I've heard somebody describe it as recovering their self … getting their selves back to where they were; not so much back to how they were before they were using, but just getting back in touch with their self.*'

This idea of recovery as not going back to the same place but re-connecting with a deeper personal 'self' is consistent with the idea that recovery is not about becoming symptom-free, but rather it is a journey to a better self. The transformation to a recovery process is not only experienced as 'from' something but also 'to' – thus one participant described this as *'Right now … I see myself as a different person, a new person, a better person and can relate to a lot of people differently than what I did when I was on drugs.'* Although the journey is often seen as incomplete, the transformation and contrast is often experienced as an active and vivid change process. And as shown in the example above, the barometer of success is measured in terms of social engagement and activity where connectedness is a marker of recovery progress.

Social network change and recovery

A consistent and dominant theme was the importance of other people in both inspiring and sustaining the recovery journey. While participants cited different types of support as being helpful, social contact or 'being with others' was a consistent and recurring theme. Several participants said that they were given hope by the example of others, often peers in recovery: *'That was where I first got hope when I see people six months, six years clean, and it sounded as though they had been through the same experience as me, the same drugs, same ways of using'.* As one participant put it, *'I thought, "Well, if they can do it, I can do it"'.* These are vivid examples of social learning and the impact that coming into contact with peers who have made the transition to recovery can have in inspiring the belief that recovery is a reality and one that can be achieved. In the examples of this social learning one key component is the viability of the comparison – in other words, for a recovery champion to act as a role model, the person has to identify with them – *'that they have been through the same as I have and if they can do it so can I'.* This is a key component of a peer model of recovery in which identification may constitute an essential prerequisite for social learning to occur, as well as the perceived attractiveness of the recovery behaviour.

However, the initiation of the recovery journey is only the first point at which peers can play a highly significant role. Many participants felt that a key factor in sustaining their recovery was mixing with people who did not use alcohol or heroin: *'keeping sober company'.* This is also characterised as a change in social networks. Several former heroin users said they had moved away from former acquaintances: *'The associates I had when I was using drugs, I'm no longer in contact with. I met new friends and they've helped me a lot'.* The change in social networks, and by implication in activities, in values, in expectations and in personal and social identity is both about moving away from former using colleagues and moving towards those who have the same aims and aspirations. The sense of a dynamic relationship between social change and personal beliefs and expectations is addressed in the following quotation:

'I'd got clean loads of times in the past for small periods, but it was just about putting the drugs down. It wasn't changing my behaviour or my thinking, doing any personal development. So this time ... my peers giving me suggestions and being open to them and being honest with myself and breaking the denial and doing a lot of self-reflecting.'

The peer is both the source of affirmation and of social learning – they provide the evidence of the success of recovery strategies but also the social space in which the person in recovery can explore and develop their skills and capabilities. The above quotation also provides a sense of the dynamic between the growth of social recovery capital (the peers and the advice and support they offer) and the growth of personal recovery capital in reflection and being honest with yourself as a core part of the recovery process.

The impact of trigger events on recovery capital

The notion of a dynamic and virtuous circle is summed up in the experience that *'I started doing voluntary work in a wee project that I came through and that's been really good ... it's good for my self-esteem, which was really low before.'* The 'recovery spin' that will be explored in this model is based on the idea that engaging in positive social networks that are active in rewarding and fulfilling activities has a dynamic effect – doing these things increases self-esteem and self-confidence that in turn increases the person's ability to be socially confident and engaged, and that this in turn increases the access to positive opportunities. The person becomes more social and becomes more active, which impacts on their self-esteem and their social capital, generating a form of confidence that makes the person like themselves more and be more open to the idea of being liked and valuing their social status and identity. The impact of this in terms of the overall model for recovery change is outlined in the concluding section of this chapter. This also relates to the social identity model (Jetten *et al*, 2009) in that membership of a recovery group affords not only social support and affirmation but also a sense of belonging and engagement that promotes recovery values and the resulting activities that in turn support recovery progress.

A second participant reported that '*Mainly what it was ... was thinking back before and how different you feel, as if you are something and how confident you are*'. That sense of change is a crucial component of the 'recovery identity' that emerges as the person feels a new sense of hope and confidence, that is contrasted with the addict self. This emerging recovery self is expressed as a contrast to the using self in a way that is framed in positive characteristics and attributes that provide the spur and impetus for further growth.

Overview and preliminary conclusions – a dynamic model of 'recovery spin'

Ronel and Elisha (2011) have written about the 'spin' of an escalating criminal career where one adverse event can trigger a series of activities and experiences that propel the person into a phase of activities and experiences that are out of control. This is a developmental model where key events act as turning points that can lead to rapid and dynamic escalations of both risk behaviours and positive recovery-oriented behaviours.

The core concept that will be explored in this account of recovery journeys of a group of people who have achieved sustained recovery is that there is an equivalent 'recovery spin' that underpins the concept of developmental and dynamic recovery capital growth in those in recovery. Within this model, personal and social capital grow as part of a dynamic of change that also alters the relationship to community or cultural capital, and this change is related to self-identity both as a personal and as a social form of identity.

This model has been articulated in mental health recovery research by Dingle *et al* (2012) in a study of assertive linkage to choir singing in a group of individuals with entrenched mental health problems. The experience of the participants is of an initial increase in personal capital (categorised as 'personal impact' by Dingle and her colleagues) through improved self-esteem and improved emotional regulation, linking to improvements in social engagement and social networks ('social impact' in the model) and finally increases in community resources and capital ('functional outcomes'), as shown in **figure 3.1**.

Figure 3.1: Changes in personal, social and functional outcomes resulting from engagement in meaningful activities

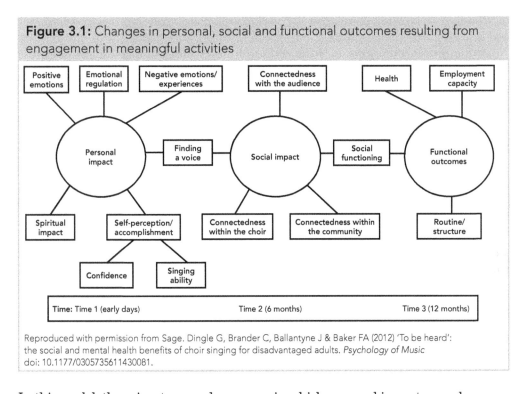

Reproduced with permission from Sage. Dingle G, Brander C, Ballantyne J & Baker FA (2012) 'To be heard': the social and mental health benefits of choir singing for disadvantaged adults. *Psychology of Music* doi: 10.1177/0305735611430081.

In this model, there is a temporal sequence in which personal impact precedes social impact, which in turn precedes functional outcomes. Because this is a study of assertive linkage, in which clinicians actively engage clients in meaningful activity, the activity precedes the benefits. Our model would suggest that this may be atypical and that it is changes in social networks and engagement that enable the initiation of meaningful activities, and this in turn cements the social network and the cycle of 'recovery spin'. The other key aspect of the model outlined by Dingle *et al* (2012) is that it provides a set of testable hypotheses around the relationship between personal and social impact and domains for measuring change – size of social network, self-esteem, and so on.

To reframe this model in terms of the current model of developmental recovery founded in positive social identity change and growing recovery capital, the three primary components remain intact, albeit in a different order:

1. **Social recovery capital:** Engaging with recovery champions and recovery groups provides social support and a sense of well-being, access to recovery role models that allow for the social learning of the techniques of recovery and the incorporation of the norms, values and beliefs of recovery.

2. **Personal recovery capital:** This safe social space provides the foundations and the conditions that enable the growth of the personal skills and resources – communication skills, self-esteem, self-efficacy, resilience skills and so on – that can be tested and refined in the safe spaces of the recovery groups.

3. **Community recovery capital:** What is particularly important about the third phase of the model is the idea that the extension of social networks – through bridging social capital to new and different groups – offers increased awareness of, and access to, resources that exist in the community. Thus, while the access to community resources among the disenfranchised and socially excluded addict communities are likely to be extremely limited, the access to new social groups and networks is likely to broaden the individual's horizons and so their capacity to take advantage of opportunities in the community.

Also critical from this model in relation to community recovery capital is the role that the dynamic growth of personal and social capital has on accessing resources in the community. It is hypothesised that the downward spiral of addiction is associated with adverse experiences of stigma and discrimination that will often be internalised (*'I am an addict and not worthy of respect or trust'*) that leads to exclusion from non-using family and friends and an increasingly exclusive social identity based on addict status, with a social network dominated by others in the same situation. This has an impact on community capital in that the excluded individual is not only likely not to find out about opportunities in their local community, they are likely to self-exclude from those opportunities, even if they do become aware of them.

In contrast, the expansion of the social network through choir-singing opens up opportunities for the development of new networks, through which informational resources as well as emotional and social support emerge. As a diverse range of individuals and groups interact with the person in recovery, so their access to community resources also grows (Putnam, 2000). In our own equivalent of the choir project, Landale and Best (2012) evaluated the impact of participation in exercise, and particularly membership of a football team, on social capital in young offenders who had not been willing to engage in traditional drug treatment. In this project, called Second Chance, the young men were offered the chance to play football as part of a team as part of their criminal justice conditions. For those who embraced this offer, the key benefits of participating were a:

- positive identity including a sense of self-efficacy
- positive self-perceptions of physical health and well-being
- positive social networks resulting from positive role models
- sense of hope and positive vision of the future.

For the young men who engaged in the football team, participation was a catalyst to a 'recovery spin' where the football not only occupied their time, but conferred on them a social role and status, a sense of purpose and dignity, a chance to do something they liked that they could be good at, and the expansion of their social networks to include people not involved in substance use and offending. Through this expanded network some members of the team were able to access opportunities for new places to live, for courses and vocational opportunities, and for participation in other footballing and leisure activities. The Second Chance project created an opportunity for a positive recovery spin in which personal and social capital rose, which in turn generated opportunities for, and the capacity to accept, community resources and capital from which they would previously have been excluded.

As the recruits to the Second Chance programme were substance-using offenders typically from the most excluded and deprived communities in the northeast of England, their social networks were likely to be restricted to other people in a similar situation. Thus, the football team opportunity afforded three things – an opportunity to develop social networks of other people in recovery, a chance to develop contacts and relationships with people from different locations and experiences, and through this linking social capital to access community capital in the form of information and access to community resources.

The model that is tested in the remainder of the book is based on the experiences of two recovery populations – people participating in a brief study of recovery trajectories and a group of people in long-term recovery who will describe their pathways into first addiction and then recovery and will look at their recovery journeys, to identify evidence for a recovery spin in which personal, social and community recovery capital emerge from opportunistic tipping points that create a virtual circle of personal growth, a new personal and social identity, and an ability to access and take advantage of community resources.

References

Best D, Ghufran S, Day E, Ray R & Loaring J (2008) Breaking the habit: a retrospective analysis of desistance factors among formerly problematic heroin users. *Drug and Alcohol Review* **27** 619–624.

Best D, Gow J, Taylor A, Knox T, Groshkova T & White W (2011a) Mapping the recovery stories of drinkers and drug users in Glasgow: quality of life and its associations with measures of recovery capital. *Drug and Alcohol Review* **31** (3) 334–341.

Best D, Gow J, Taylor A, Knox A & White W (2011b) Recovery from heroin or alcohol dependence: a qualitative account of the recovery experience in Glasgow. *Journal of Drug Issues* **11** (1) 359–378.

Dingle G, Brander C, Ballantyne J & Baker FA (2012) 'To be heard': the social and mental health benefits of choir singing for disadvantaged adults. *Psychology of Music* doi: 10.1177/0305735611430081.

Hibbert L & Best D (2011) Assessing recovery and functioning in former problem drinkers at different stages of their recovery journeys. *Drug and Alcohol Review* **30** 12–20.

Jetten J, Haslam SA, Iyer A & Haslam C (2009) Turning to others in times of change: shared identity and coping with stress. In: S Stürmer and M Snyder (Eds) *New Directions in the Study of Helping: Group-level perspectives on motivations, consequences and interventions* (pp 139–156). Chichester: Wiley-Blackwell.

Landale S & Best D (2012) Dynamic shifts in social networks and normative values in recovery from an offending and drug using lifestyle (p219-236). In: CD Johnston (Ed) *Social Capital: Theory, measurement and outcomes*. New York: Nova Science Publishers Inc.

Laudet A, Morgen K & White W (2006) The role of social supports, spirituality, religiousness, life meaning and affiliation with 12-step fellowships in quality of life satisfaction among individuals in recovery from alcohol and drug problems. *Alcohol Treatment Quarterly* **24** 33–73.

Longabaugh R, Wirtz P, Zywiak W & O'Malley S (2010) Network support as a prognostic indicator of drinking outcomes: The COMBINE study. *Journal of Studies on Alcohol and Drugs* **71** (6) 837–846.

Putnam R (2000) *Bowling Alone: The collapse and revival of American community*. New York: Simon and Schuster.

Ronel N & Elisha E (2011) A different perspective: introducing positive criminology. *International Journal of Offender Therapy and Comparative Criminology* **2** 305–325.

Skevington SM, Lotfy M & O'Connell KA (2004) The World Health Organization's WHOQOL-BREF quality of life assessment: psychometric properties and results of the international field trial. A report from the WHOQOL group. *Quality of Life Research* **13** 299–310.

Chapter 4: Pilot stories of recovery

What is in a word, and what is in a story?

Recovery narratives offer a wonderful opportunity for individuals to describe the incredible achievement that is recovery from addiction. They constitute a very particular kind of action that acknowledges – either implicitly or explicitly – a transition from a pre-recovery state that many will refer to as 'active addiction' – to something else. What that something else is remains at the heart of the mystery of recovery, and incorporates many of the debates about definition.

For some people this is a shedding of an old identity and a moving into a new phase of life where addiction plays a relatively insignificant part. However, for many others, in particular the advocates of a 12-step philosophy, recovery is a process of ongoing change where the former status, 'addict', is not discarded, rather it is qualified by 'recovering'. This is at the heart of the question of whether people choose to classify themselves as 'recovered' (something I once was but am no longer) or 'recovering' (something that I still am in the process of overcoming). However, it is not the case that those in recovery are grouping themselves as part of the same group as active addicts.

This has fundamental implications for identity, with two major implications for the interpretation of this report. Those who describe themselves as 'recovering' may well be aligning themselves with the 12-step movement and the underlying assumption that addiction is a disease which, if you are unfortunate enough to be afflicted by, you will never overcome, and your recovery prefix implies that you have managed to control the symptoms, not achieve a cure. In contrast, for those who describe themselves as 'recovered', this may be a rejection (conscious or unconscious) of the 12-step philosophy. This would be the position that would be taken by many of those whose route to recovery is through the therapeutic community movement and at a recent conference in the Gold Coast in Australia, Rowdy Yates (ATCA Conference presentation, October 2013) outlined the following argument for rejecting the 12-step position.

Yates argued that part of the reason why addiction is stigmatised results from the perception that it is a lifelong disease. He argued that the reason people do not want to live next door to recovering addicts is that they are diseased for life and so the neighbourhood can never know when they will 'fall off the wagon' and return to their drinking and using ways. Yates compared this to the rationale of methadone maintenance prescribing by suggesting both contribute to stigma by inferring that cure is not possible and so only a tenuous grip on sobriety is attained (in one model by maintaining a prescription and in the other by maintaining attendance at 12-step meetings). This is a highly charged and emotive issue that is but one manifestation of the enormous shadow that the 12-step movement casts over the world of recovery. While there is a clear group identity that differentiates the 'recovering addict' from the 'active addict', there is an overt recognition of the possibility that regression to the active stage will occur without vigilance. Within the fellowships, this is an important distinction that may be much less meaningful to other members of the community who may not have the knowledge or experience to make the distinction (or to care about the gradations within the stigmatised label of 'addict'). Within the context of the fellowship, this may be a salient identity but the broader category of addict may well have a greater impact in the wider social context. This in turn may result in an unwillingness to disclose addict status.

Yet the 'recovering addict' identity is a powerful identity for those who have embraced the 12 steps of the fellowships. Recovery narratives are often replete with stock phrases – 'one day at a time', 'rock bottom' and 'dry drunk' to name but three – and they can readily be interpreted as communication of membership as much as a person describing themselves as a 'friend of Bill W'. The deployment of such phrases – which has been a common feature of the recovery studies I have been involved in both in the UK and in Australia – are indicative of both the internalisation of the worldview of the group (Haslam *et al*, 2008) and of their acceptance of its applicability to their own recovery story. No similar narrative structure is apparent in the recovery stories of those in recovery who have come through the other recovery tradition, that of the therapeutic community.

But the shadow of 12-step has another consequence in that, for many people, the use of the word, in the context of alcohol or illicit drugs, is a concession to the discourse of 12-step. This influences not only where research participants will place themselves in relation to the 'in recovery/recovered' dichotomy, but also their willingness to engage with a research project that describes itself as being about recovery. This has interesting implications in the original social identity model and in particular self-categorisation theory (Tajfel & Turner, 1979). By definition, agreeing to take part in a project about recovery stories assumes that the participant both recognises the legitimacy of the term and its application to them, and that they will overtly apply that label to themselves.

This has critical implications for the sample who will be engaged in the research project. As the population of people in recovery is not known, it is very difficult to gauge how representative those taking part in any research study might be. Thus, while the 'natural recovery' work of Granfield and Cloud (1996) suggests that it is possible to access populations not engaged in recovery-supportive networks, there is likely to be a disproportionate representation of people who are readily accessed for projects like the collation of recovery narratives. There are two primary reasons for this – ease of recruitment through established recovery groups and the resulting 'word of mouth' dissemination of awareness about and information on the project. In our experience in the UK, it has been much easier to recruit via visible recovery groups and communities and attempts to recruit through advertising have not been particularly successful.

However, there is an additional issue that arises from describing the project as related to 'recovery' in that it places the discourse in a frame that is familiar and comfortable to individuals with certain belief systems, including advocates of the 12-step movement. Thus, there is always the risk that, while AA and NA will never advocate or recruit on behalf of a research project, that such projects end up recruiting disproportionately from the mutual aid groups and the aftercare communities connected to the therapeutic communities.

Recovery populations

There is some movement – particularly in the US – to use population surveys to improve our capacity to estimate recovery at a population level. In 2013, White *et al* were successful in having recovery questions included in a general population health survey and reported that 9.45% of the general adult population in Philadelphia self-reported that they were in recovery from an alcohol or drug problem. While the authors focused on the relative health and economic disadvantages experienced by this group, they were also keen to emphasise what a significant constitution of recovering adults this represented.

Earlier in the same year, Faces and Voices of Recovery (FAVOR) published the results of their Life in Recovery (2013) survey, recruiting more than 3,000 people to complete a survey assessing the change from active addiction to recovery – with marked improvements reported in physical and psychological health, community contribution, improvements in employment and family engagement, and reductions in offending, criminal justice system involvement and health service utilisation. But the same problems beset this project as other retrospective recovery studies:

- people are both self-selecting as having had an addiction problem and as currently not having one
- they are self-identifying as being in recovery and so classifying themselves as people who have made this transition.

However, crucially, from the perspective of recovery stories, they are also engaging in a public action around being overt about their recovery status. While studies will vary in the extent to which they will promise or commit to anonymity for participants, participation in a recovery project is a kind of public act that proclaims a set of assumptions about recovery and about the individual's own understanding of what recovery means and is about.

Recruiting and engaging people in a recovery project

In research studies of this kind, where the population of those in recovery is hard to estimate or characterise (inevitably it excludes those who do not want to discuss their journey, who would not characterise their life in terms of such a transition and more prosaically, those who simply cannot be contacted), sampling is a challenge for researchers. This is based on the fear that the experiences of those participating are not 'representative' or typical in ways that skew or distort the themes identified and the conclusions reached. With the work of White *et al* (2013) in Pennsylvania there are increasing options of starting to describe the population based on epidemiological survey work, but this work remains at a relatively early stage.

Primarily, this limitation in research methods has often resulted in the fear that the 'voice' of 12-step is heard more loudly than competing pathways to recovery and so is seen as the prime path to recovery. While this pilot cannot overcome this concern, the pilot data presented in the remainder of this chapter used a primarily online recruitment method in an attempt to broaden the sample of those recruited, with no attempt to use any existing contacts to generate a sample of respondents, and no overt snowballing techniques employed. It is also new in that it is the first time that I have been involved in the collection of recovery stories that involve gambling as well as alcohol and illicit drugs – but again with the same starting point of actively encouraging participation from anyone who regards themselves as being in recovery, with no preliminary screening involved, and no assumptions about the stage of the recovery journey the participant had achieved.

As in previous studies I have led, the inclusion criteria were still basically that a person had a lifetime addiction and that they perceive themselves to have been in recovery for at least one year. This has generally been operationalised by specifying that the person has not used their primary substance in the last year (or for gambling, has not gambled in this period). However, when I have been approached by people to ask if they were able to take part, I have been happy to relax these criteria for individuals who wanted to be part of the project. This is not consistent with good research practice but has a much more important action and ethical research component that adheres to the recovery principle of inclusivity.

This relates to telling a story. One of the most wonderful things about recovery research is that it affords an individual the opportunity to tell their story – and, while for some this will be a practiced narrative, for others it will be the first time they have had that opportunity. For that reason, the work presented in this chapter is in response to a limited series of prompts. Those prompts are designed to ensure that the story is told from a 'developmental life course' perspective but to ensure that the individual owns their own story and can frame the key aspects of their story in a language that makes sense to them. In each of the chapters in this book, I have tried to both provide a flavour of the diversity of experiences that constitute recovery journeys but also to convey the sense of wonder and gratitude that flavour the stories that are told.

In the case of the stories presented in this chapter, I have had relatively little control over what those stories look like. After some piloting through the Eastern Health Consumer and Carer Advisory Council, the dissemination of this project was via word of mouth and those accessing the Turning Point website in Australia, and was done in part of a process to establish a recovery page on the Turning Point website. Turning Point is a major treatment, training and research centre in Victoria, Australia, where I have been fortunate enough to work as Head of Research and Workforce Development in recent years, and who have increasingly been supportive of and engaged in the transitions to a recovery-oriented approach.

So other than to thank the participants who contributed to this project, there is very little I can say about them – I do not have demographic characteristics or backgrounds and I know nothing about where or when or why they completed the survey, but as will be apparent later in this text, they are also a group whose diversity means that some of the previous concerns about sampling techniques do not apply. These are the stories of recovery of a diverse group of people who responded to an online request for recovery stories.

Short stories of recovery

The brief instructions asked participants five questions:

- Briefly describe your drinking, using or gambling history.
- What caused you to reduce or stop your drinking, drug use or gambling?
- What factors have helped you to stay in recovery?
- What does recovery mean for you?
- What is your life like now?

The aim was to characterise the journeys of people who perceive themselves to be recovered or in recovery and very little instruction was given to potential participants, and they were not asked to provide any more information other than their gender, age and their occupation. However, to ensure that anonymity is preserved, the data will be presented by case number with gender and age added, where the participant has offered that information. In the sections below, themes that emerged in relation to each of the five questions. This follows in the developmental tradition outlined by Hser (2007) and aims to explore narrative reports of turning points in the addiction and recovery careers, and the Ronel and Elisha (2011) concept of 'spin' by examining the impact of a major life event (stopping use) on subsequent lifestyle and life events.

Fifty individuals completed the brief online survey – some with only a paragraph and others with extensive and detailed stories, with the key findings summarised below and outlined according to the key stages of the recovery journey.

Briefly describe your drinking, using or gambling history

For some people, the onset of problems could be linked to a core event, thus, participant #1 (female, 52) reported that *'after a horrific experience … Of harassment, discrimination, foul play and closed ranks of an academic department at an Australian university, I developed a drinking problem'*. Another, participant #33 (female, 39) reported that *'I started binge drinking in my late 20s after ending an emotionally and physically abusive relationship'*.

Finally, participant #29 told their story as '*I was introduced to heroin at 18, and maintained casual or occasional use until aged 23 when I met and fell in love with a dealer. I lived the dream for over a year until he was jailed, and I was not only forced to hang out alone (none of my family, friends or colleagues knew we were users) but I was also forced, for the first time, to choose how I would support a habit in the future*'. In these instances, the turning point for the initiation of substance problems is traced to a particular event or sequence of events that represented a negative turning point.

However, for many it was not an event but a response to life circumstances that initiated addiction problems. Thus, participant #18 (female, 45) reported that '*I grew up in families that had a lot of addiction issues and from an early age I have been experimenting with drugs*'. The idea of family influences also occurred in the report of participant #43 (female, 53) who reported that '*I started drinking at 15, and stopped just before my 45th birthday. Nearly 30 years, it got progressively worse. My family is riddled with the disease of alcoholism*'. A third participant reported that '*I was self-medicating with cannabis and painkillers for years, trying to feel normal*'. In these instances, the narrative is of an adverse trajectory that created both the conditions and the opportunity to engage in harmful substance use.

Others did not attempt to explain but rather to describe the progression in their substance-using career – participant #5 reported that '*at age 17, I started smoking marijuana, dabbled in heroin by age 19, having been introduced to this via the smoking crowd. In my 20s I did some speed, in my late 20s binge drinking and by my mid-30s a full-blown heroin addiction started*'. Similarly, participant #10 (female, 32) reported that '*I started drinking and smoking cigarettes and pot [cannabis] aged 12. I used LSD and ecstasy during my teenage years. I used magic mushrooms heavily for a year when I was 27 and then used heroin*'. Participant #22 (male, 48) reported that '*I started drinking at 13 and gambling at 16 – since then I have always gambled and I am always broke*'. These are stories of escalation in which the individual describes increases in either the severity or the riskiness of their substance-using behaviour.

The careers described were often lengthy in duration and often involved a range of substances, causes and social circumstances. As in previous studies, there is no common cause or pathways to substance problems or gambling problems but a personal story that is sometimes around life choices and sometimes in response to problems in the home or in personal well-being. This variability is also reflected in the factors described as reasons for wanting or attempting to put an end to substance use. Before going on to describe these, it is important to make one critical point about the philosophy of recovery, at least as it is promoted by most credible recovery researchers. And that is that there is no assumption that everyone does or should aspire to, or achieve recovery. For all the stories presented in this and subsequent chapters, recovery is seen as a personal choice and a life transition that only some people will feel the need or desire to make. This book is for those who have made that choice or for those working with and supporting those who have made the choice to aspire to recovery. In other words, the accounts here, however brief, are presented by those comfortable with the concept of recovery and who see it as having a relevance and meaning in their own life narrative.

What caused you to stop or reduce your substance use?

As with all of the questions asked, responses came from a range of perspectives and covered a wide array of domains. The aim of this section is to explore the triggers to a recovery journey and this follows from previous research on recovery (Best *et al*, 2008) showing that the events that initiated a recovery journey (which are more typically to do with cumulative fatigue with the lifestyle) are different from those that sustain recovery (which are more typically social).

Participant #1 (female, 52) reported that '*I have reduced significantly over the years, including periods of abstinence [from alcohol] in the quest to have a greater sense of well-being*'. For participant #3 (male, 47) the issue was more of a cumulative effect '*I was sick and tired of being sick and tired*'. This is interesting in two senses – the first that it coheres with an effect previously reported (Best *et al*, 2008) that there is a cumulative effect as individuals experience developmental change to the point of wanting to 'mature out'. However, it is also interesting in that this is a statement that is widely used in 12-step discourse and is a standard part of the narrative. As discussed above, it is both part of the dialogue of change but it is also an acknowledgement and a warrant of membership.

This sense of life having no purpose or pleasure was summed up by participant #6 (female, 49) who explained '*I was isolating myself totally, cancelling meetings with friends, not going on family outings so that I could stay home and drink… after cancelling another meeting, my best friend told me our friendship was over after 38 years, so I went round to her house and told her I was an alcoholic*'. The sense of cumulative effect is also summed up in the experience of participant #8 (male, 50) who said that '*Nothing stopped me for a long, long time. It didn't matter that my friends were dropping off, or my wife and daughter had left. I still had two good jobs. I could find company when it took my fancy… The slap in the face came when my health and appearance started to suffer'*. Finally, participant #11 (female, 55) reported along the same lines that *'It wasn't one thing but a number of things – my kids, my job, sick of the life I was leading'*.

However, the cumulative 'falling out of love' with the substance and the cumulative effect on well-being and lifestyle were often accompanied by trigger events. Pregnancy was one such event – participant #18 reported that *'I fell pregnant and so I was in touch with the Royal Women's – for me it was impossible to use with another human inside me. I felt it was my choice to wreck my life but not to inflict it on a child'*. A similar event trigger was reported by participant #32 (female, 38) who reported that *'my children were taken away from me for one month'*. Similarly, participant #28 reported that *'I ended up having a psychiatric episode and I tried to overdose on the painkillers and get myself admitted to hospital so I could get enough tablets'*. The combination of these cumulative and event triggers are summed up by participant #31 (female, 43) who said that *'I was working as a prostitute and my daughter had to go to live with her father full-time, and people were starting to close doors on me. One of the biggest rock bottoms was when my front tooth fell out and I realised how awful I looked'*.

For many people, the transition to recovery is not a straightforward one and can take a number of episodes – but this is not always the case. Participant #42 reported that *'My life was physically and mentally destroyed. I wanted to die and didn't know how to live. I went to AA and learned that I was an alcoholic and what that meant, and how to live a happy and joyous life without alcohol'*. A more common experience is the gradual and learned transition to recovery, as reported by participant #45 (female, 45) who reported that *'when I was 27, I spent New Year with my brother and his girlfriend, doing coke on my own because I was too paranoid and unable to go out. I ended up in bed by 11pm in the foetal position thinking I was going to have a heart attack and hating myself. I went to my first Narcotics Anonymous meeting two days later. I didn't stop completely that day, it took another 16 months for me to quit drugs completely'*.

This last case study is a good example of the complexity of the desistance trigger – that stopping is often a gradual process rather than a sudden event, with the initial decision to stop resulting in changes in lifestyle and behaviour that enable the initiation of the recovery journey. Because for many people, addiction has become all-encompassing in their lives, recovery necessitates major life changes that go beyond putting down the bottle or drugs that may involve changes in housing and employment, but crucially in relationships and friendship networks.

What factors have helped you to stay in recovery?

In our 2008 paper (Best *et al*, 2008) we concluded that the factors that allow people to stop are not the factors that support people to initiate and maintain a recovery journey, and that the maintenance factors are much more likely to be social factors. This principle of recovery is borne out in the current study. It is also consistent with the analysis of White (2009) that recovery is a journey that takes place over time and that 'stable recovery' (UKDPC, 2008) may take as long as five years to achieve.

For participant #3 (male, 47) there was a combination of social effects and the benefits of 12-step engagement that were seen as critical to sustaining recovery, *'Being surrounded by people sharing the same aims ... working at recovery. Attending meetings'*. A similar combination was reported by participant #11 (female, 55) who cited *'family support, NA and me not wanting to go back there'* as the factors that enabled her to sustain recovery. The mutual aid fellowships were often referred to in this kind of combination typified by participant #14 (female, 32) who reported *'Family support, good relationships and regular appointments with my drug counsellor. Becoming a member of Narcotics Anonymous; enrolling in study; moving into private rental; not associating with drug users (deleting phone numbers and people from Facebook)'*. Not all recovery participation involves 12-step (in fact, less than half of those who provided narratives cited mutual aid group involvement) however, participant #22 (male, 48) reported that his recovery was sustained by *'joining groups involved in recovery, and being more involved in community and arts projects – voluntary work is most important for awareness and education'*. For many people, there is no single method or technique and that recovery is about building a life that involves connections and a sense of purpose and belonging.

For others, the social support was not affiliated to recovery groups but to family. Participant #5 (female, 51) reported that what helped her stay in recovery was *'My family and a clean, warm, safe place to sleep far away from the inner city'*, reflecting that combination of social capital in the form of family and avoiding the people and places that would trigger use. She goes on to describe this journey, *'I am with my son and it has given me the opportunity to engage in psychotherapy for the last two years and become part of the Pathways to Exit programme for ex sex workers'*. The sense of important others as providing both a motive for recovery and an anchor for the ongoing journey and challenges was a common theme in the recovery stories provided.

The theme of family was also critical to participant #28 (female, 49) who reported that her recovery was sustained by '*A beautiful, young, adult daughter ... and an encouraging husband who has seen me in good times and at my worst*'. Similarly, another female respondent (#10, aged 32) described recovery factors as '*Support from my family and friends. Suitable medication for my depression and mental illness. My wish to be a present and attentive mother. Great GP and counsellor who I see on a regular basis. Exercise and good diet*'. For this participant, there is an ongoing story of change and struggle but embedded within a family and professional network of support. I will return to a theme that has become apparent in writing this book – the significant differences in the recovery journeys of men and women. This is consistent with the writing of Cheong *et al* (2013) in that health care professionals represent a key part of the community recovery capital and that this is a fundamental component of the recovery support network.

Connection was a dominant theme as reported by participant #31 (female, 43) '*I have stayed in recovery because of the connection that I have with other people in recovery. My life has improved so much that I don't see any reason to change what I am doing*'. Similarly, participant #36 (female, 37) sustained recovery by '*Surrounding myself with like-minded drug-free people ... breaking free from negative people and influences in my life*'. The effect that we reported in the addiction professionals' project in 2008 also chimes with the effect reported by Longabaugh *et al* (2010) from the COMBINE study where the generation of a positive social network supportive of recovery is critical to the recovery journey.

For a small number of people the salient factors took the form of a personal journey where others were not prominent. Thus, participant #13 reported '*Learning to know myself and care about myself... Learning to educate myself about triggers, cravings and knowing when to seek support. I found study and focused upon my values in life to be integral to my recovery*'. This personal motivation was reflected by participant #15 (female, 33) who stated that '*My main motivation is within myself and I have little or no external reasons or pressures. And besides all of this, my experience is that life is more enjoyable when I am abstinent*'.

The final word on this will go to participant #44 (female, 48) who listed the key factors in sustaining her recovery '*Support; counselling, giving back to the community; volunteering; art therapy; healthy diet and exercise; training and education; financial guidance; keeping busy; developing self-worth and being kind to myself*'. Maintaining recovery is a complex process but the answers here are entirely in keeping with those reported in previous recovery studies I have been involved in (Best *et al*, 2008; Best *et al*, 2011a; Best *et al*, 2011b):

- involvement in recovery groups, including but not restricted to 12-step groups
- re-engagement with the family
- developing new social networks
- moving away from using networks
- engaging in meaningful activities (including volunteering and paid employment)
- developing personal strengths and inner resources.

What does recovery mean for you, and what is your life like now?

In the final section of this review of the online recovery stories, I will examine the current state of the participants based on the final two questions – 'what is your life like now?' and 'what does recovery mean for you?'

Participant #1 (female, 52) provides a wonderful definition. *'Recovery is a journey; a life full of meaning and purpose; healthy relationships; inner peace and calm; radiating the joy of God and positive loved ones in my life; personal growth and development; helping others on their journey and volunteer work to help the marginalised in society'*. Participant #3 (male, 47) is more succinct in his description of recovery as *'Freedom, life, integrity'* and his own life as *'Like anyone else's – except perhaps the ups and downs are a little harsher. Nothing special – but a good life'*.

The notion of a normal life is critical in the discourse of recovery. Participant #6 (female, 49) said that *'It means I have my life back, my recovery comes first and foremost. It means I am reliable and do what I say I am going to do, I am completely free to be who I am and to live the best life I possibly can. I am happier now than I have ever been and feel each day sober is a blessing and I am so grateful for every moment'*. This is entirely consistent with a word that has been suggested as a better alternative to 'recovery'. It is the Greek word 'eudaimonia', which means human flourishing, and was described by Aristotle as the highest good for human beings. It is this sense of recovery that is critical – that it is not a perfect life, but a meaningful and a fulfilled one that is normal and human but is about growth and achievement. The above quotations do not mention alcohol or drugs or addiction, rather they talk about growth and well-being and integrity, and are framed in the everyday struggles of life.

Thus, participant #13 (female, 48) describes her current life as '*My relationships, with those I love are great and most importantly my relationship with myself is going well*', and this is consistent with a view of recovery as '*...being able to live life in line with my values and life vision. I can now feel the highs and lows in life. I am no longer numb. It is a great feeling knowing that I can make choices in life*'.

This journey is not without ongoing pain for many people. Participant #5 (female, 51) describes her life as, '*I am strong, I am intelligent and I will never stop trying to navigate my way back to life but I would be lying if I said it was easy. It wasn't until I stopped that I realised what I had forfeited and what underlying problems had led me into a life of pain and addiction*'. A similar perception arose in the response of participant #10 (female, 32), '*Still I have hard times, however, I can deal with hardship and crisis without using drugs. I have a positive outlook for the future. I am not always happy but that is OK as I have accepted that life will have good and bad times and I can deal with that in a healthy way. I am a good mum, partner, daughter and sister. We can pay the bills, buy food and other necessities when we need to*'. In this quotation, the sense of reality and perspective blends with a sense of belonging and connectedness, to others and to her own reality.

The sense of reciprocity is a critical factor for a number of respondents. Participant #18 (female, 18) felt that '*Recovery means having an enjoyable and productive life – being a part of something and putting in to help others*'. Similarly, participant #20 (female, 58) defined recovery, for her, as '*being abstinent from alcohol, reconnecting to the world, maintaining relationships and being able to function in my daily life*'. The reciprocal experience was also described by participant #32 (female, 38) as '*Living life to the fullest with clear thoughts and perception. Associating with like-minded people that have goals and put things in place. Understanding that nothing is impossible – helping others now that I can and have helped myself*'.

Likewise, participant #21 (male, 43) describes life in recovery as, '*I enjoy a beautiful relationship with my daughters and I have a healthy and loving relationship with my partner. I can work, I am useful, I wake up every morning through sober eyes. The most important thing is that I can live and deal with whatever life throws at me, good and bad*'. Connection is also critical for participant #30 (female, 33) who describes her life as '*Better than it was and improving all the time thanks to the loving help, support and guidance from those around me*'.

There is a remarkable sense of wonder and joy in many of the stories, particularly around where people are currently in their lives. Participant #23 (female, 40) describes this as, '*My life is amazing. I never thought I could find happiness or peace, but I have got them. People love me, trust me. People can depend on me. I have integrity, I have faith. I don't live in fear or loneliness or resentment. It is awesome*'. Participant 36 (female, 37) reports that '*I am such a positive person now who takes nothing for granted and I am truly grateful for everything I have with my amazing husband and two beautiful boys. I take pride and comfort in knowing that what I feel that I missed out on as a child I have a chance to correct with my children ... I am happy, I am healthy, I am loved and I love deeply*'.

Addiction research is full of stories of misery and pain, yet the stories here tell of a very different experience and trajectory for people who can make the transition to lasting and stable recovery. It is not everyone who will make this transition, and the sober life will not be without pain or problems, but the current experiences tell of a re-birth, a connectedness and a transition to an entirely different way of being. One of the key themes in the quotations above is that the recovery experience is about getting on with life and there is very little reference to substances or the symptoms of craving, withdrawal or drug highs. However, the addiction experience remains a key part of the life journey and in this sense can be seen as part of the growth experience of accumulating wisdom, knowledge, resilience and skills for the life journey.

Summary of the online stories

The term 'eudaimonia' has been suggested as a better alternative to recovery for one negative reason (it does not imply going back to how things were before as the word 'recovery' may) and one positive (it is about ongoing and everyday human flourishing, with the bumps and grinds that this entails).

The stories in this chapter are hard to read without a sense of awe, wonder and humility that suggests that great human adversity – not only addiction but abuse, trauma and discrimination – can be transcended. The stories are of a grounded and grateful recognition of an incredible personal journey, but one that is intrinsically bound with other people.

In 2011, along with a medical student, Louise Hibbert (Hibbert & Best, 2011), we came up with the idea that recovery is not about going back to normal levels of quality of life, but of achieving a socially embedded sense of well-being that exceeds the 'normal'. This 'better than well' phenomenon has not been studied satisfactorily, but the stories here suggest exactly this experience of transcendence and ongoing growth. There are no guarantees that bad things will not happen to the participants in the stories recounted here (they will, such is the nature of all of our lives) but that they are in the moment of their lives and experiencing a gratitude and a well-being that not only contrasts with the addicted state, but also a journey of continuing growth and hope.

In the next chapter, I will move forward to examine this process from a series of interviews and questionnaires completed by addiction professionals who see themselves as being in recovery. The same themes of transition and development will be examined and the notion of a gendered experience of recovery further explored.

References

Best D, Ghufran S, Day E, Ray R & Loaring J (2008) Breaking the habit: a retrospective analysis of desistance factors among formerly problematic heroin users. *Drug and Alcohol Review* **27** (6) 619–624.

Best D, Gow J, Taylor A, Knox T, Groshkova T & White W (2011a) Mapping the recovery stories of drinkers and drug users in Glasgow: quality of life and its associations with measures of recovery capital. *Drug and Alcohol Review* **31** (3) 334–341.

Best D, Groshkova T, Sadler J, Day E & White W (2011b) What is recovery? Functioning and recovery stories of self-identified people in recovery in a service users' group and their peer networks in Birmingham England. *Alcoholism Treatment Quarterly* **29** 293–313.

Cheong L, Armour C & Bosnich-Anticevich S (2013) Primary health care teams and the patient perspective: a social network analysis. *Research in Social and Administrative Pharmacy* http://dx.doi.org/10.1016/j.sapharm.2012.12.003.

Faces and Voices of Recovery (2013) *Life in Recovery: Report on the survey findings* [online]. Available at: http://www.facesandvoicesofrecovery.org/pdf/Life_in_Recovery_Survey3.pdf. (accessed January 2014).

Granfield R & Cloud W (1996) The elephant that nobody sees: natural recovery among middle class addicts. *Journal of Drug Issues* **26** (1) 45–61.

Haslam C, Holme A, Haslam SA, Iyer A, Jetten J & Williams WH (2008) Maintaining group memberships: social identity predicts well-being after stroke. *Neuropsychological Rehabilitation* **18** 671–691.

Hibbert L & Best D (2011) Assessing recovery and functioning in former problem drinkers at different stages of their recovery journey. *Drug and Alcohol Review* **30** 12–20.

Hser Y (2007) Predicting long-term stable recovery from heroin addiction: Findings from a 33-year follow-up study. *Journal of Addictive Diseases* **26** 51–60.

Longabaugh R, Wirtz P, Zywiak W & O'Malley S (2010) Network support as a prognostic indicator of drinking outcomes: the COMBINE study. *Journal of Studies on Alcohol and Drugs* **71** 837–846.

Ronel N & Elisha E (2011) A different perspective: introducing positive criminology. *International Journal of Offender Therapy and Comparative Criminology* **2** 305–325.

Tajfel H & Turner J (1979) An integrative theory of intergroup conflict. In: WG Austin and S Worchel (Eds) *The Social Psychology of Intergroup Relations* (p33–47). Monterey, CA: Brooks/Cole.

UK Drug Policy Commission (2008) *The UK Drug Policy Commission Recovery Consensus Group: A vision of recovery*. London: UK Drug Policy Commission and HM Government.

White WL (2009) The mobilization of community resources to support long-term addiction recovery. *Journal of Substance Abuse Treatment* **36** (2) 146–158 doi: 10.1016/j.jsat.2008.10.006.

White W, Weingartner R, Levine M, Evans A & Lamb R (2013) Recovery prevalence and health profile of people in recovery: results of a southeastern Pennsylvania survey on the resolution of alcohol and other drug problems. *Journal of Psychoactive Drugs* **45** (4) 287–296.

Chapter 5: Rationale, design and pilot studies for the professional interviews

In this chapter, the rationale for the main data collection phase will be outlined for the data that will be presented in subsequent chapters, along with the key questions asked and an outline of the instruments used to collect the data. The main part of this chapter describes a group of research participants who are deliberately unrepresentative of 'typical' recovery journeys – they are all professionals from the alcohol and drug field – primarily but not exclusively clinicians – who are in long-term recovery, and who, to varying degrees, are open about their recovery status and about their recovery journeys and pathways.

The reason for this is that part of this investigation is about the visibility of recovery champions and the experiences of overtly acknowledging a recovery status. The underlying model that is outlined here is based on a number of assumptions. In the UK Drug Strategy there is a central role for 'recovery champions' (HM Government, 2010) based on the assumption that recovery is a form of social contagion (Best, 2012) in which exposure to successful role models of recovery is an important step in the promotion and dissemination of recovery in local communities. But there is also a significant concern for many individuals that not only is substance use stigmatised but that recovery is also a stigmatised state, particularly in the workplace. Phillips and Shaw (2013) conducted a study on stigmatisation, based on 161 members of the general public reading stories about substance use, obesity and smoking where the character either had an active problem or was in remission. The authors found that not only were active users of substance more stigmatised and discriminated against, the second most stigmatised group was those in recovery from substance use. This is indicative of the problems that may be faced by individuals whose recovery status is neither supported nor celebrated by the general public.

Since moving to Australia, I have been struck by the number of professionals in the alcohol and drug field who are sympathetic to the recovery movement but who are unwilling to become involved because of their anxieties about the impact it will have on their career. Given the importance of recovery visibility to the idea of social contagion, measuring barriers to visibility is important and so one of the key themes to be addressed in this section is around adverse impact of disclosing recovery status. This is also an important barometer of the culture in professional alcohol and drug services as low levels of willingness to disclose recovery status among professionals may well be indicative of negative professional attitudes to recovery in specialist alcohol and drug treatment services.

Thus, the key assumptions that are to be tested in this section are that:

- recovery can be understood as a developmental process that takes place over time and that it is not a linear process
- recovery takes place in a socially embedded context and that it is fundamentally linked to concepts of social identity
- there are discrete stages to a recovery journey that involve acute addiction and early attempts at change that may not be successful
- there is a gradual transition to a recovery identity that is embedded in changes in social networks and social supports
- transitions into a wider journey of life exploration and growth that has nothing to do with substance use or desistance, and that involves decisions around disclosure of recovery experience that form a core component of the recovery identity.

The origins of the study

The forerunner of this study was conducted in 2008 (Best *et al*, 2008b), when we recruited from a range of sources – including a professional conference that was part of the early recovery movement in the UK. In this project, our aim was to build up a picture of recovery pathways and the instrument used was a brief questionnaire with the option for participants of providing us with their contact details for a more in-depth follow-up interview. Around 200 people completed the brief survey (of whom just under half provided details for a follow-up) with the primary research paper involving the 108 individuals who reported recovery from heroin addiction. Their stories focused particularly on two themes – the initial cessation event and the maintenance of recovery. The experiences were different – the reason given for stopping was primarily about a gradual disaffection with the drug and the related lifestyle, but often brought to a head by a catalyst event – loss of job or relationship, a health crisis or involvement with the criminal justice system. However, the factors that were associated with maintaining recovery were much more strongly linked to social networks – both in terms of moving away from the using network and actively engaging with a recovery network. For illicit drug users in particular, a complete change in location and networks was likely to be reported as a core part of the recovery journey.

This is entirely in keeping with the findings of Longabaugh *et al* (2010) who have argued that the success of Project MATCH clients was to some extent predicted by their effective transition from a social network supportive of drinking to a social network supportive of recovery. In a follow-up to our original study (Best *et al,* 2010), we also reported the very different recovery journeys for heroin users compared to drinkers with the former group typically having much less positive social capital that they could fall back on in existing networks so being more likely to need to move to new areas and new networks than former alcoholics.

To test some of these findings, the Glasgow Recovery Study was then constructed to examine these factors in much more detail. The design of the current study builds on the Glasgow Recovery Study (Best *et al,* 2011a) which is why this study is given such prominence in the previous chapter and uses a similar method of combining qualitative and quantitative data within a life-course model (as outlined by Hser *et al,* 2007). There is a core component of storytelling about this approach and, although some structured interview components are used, the overall model is basically about sense-making around stages of a recovery career. One of the main findings of both the London and Glasgow based recovery studies was the openness participants displayed about their recovery journey and the enthusiasm for telling their recovery stories. For this reason, most of the recent recovery studies have used a mixed methods approach where structured assessments of history and current well-being are followed by a semi-structured interview that encourages participants to provide a narrative account of their addiction and recovery careers.

There are six stages identified in this process and which are prompted in the semi-structured section of the interview.

1. The experience of acute addiction – why substance use started, how it escalated and why it became problematic.
2. Initial attempts at stopping and their effects – this section aims to encourage participants to reflect on initial and unsuccessful quit attempts.

3. Final and successful cessation attempt – in contrast they are then encouraged to reflect in more detail on the final and successful cessation attempt.

4. Early stages of recovery and transition to a recovery lifestyle – participants are encouraged to discuss how life changed over the course of the early recovery years.

5. Stable recovery – how long they consider they have been in stable recovery for and what this transition felt like.

6. Life as it currently is.

Recovery currency

The focus is on developmental pathways and life trajectories and the idea that recovery can be understood in biographical terms that relate to personal and social capital. This new focus on recovery capital (Granfield & Cloud, 2001) rests on two primary studies and the development of two instruments that are included in the current analysis.

In 2010, I co-authored a paper for the Royal Society for the Arts with the American researcher Alexandre Laudet on recovery capital, where we classified recovery capital in terms of three component parts:

1. **personal recovery capital:** characterised as the personal attributes and skills that individuals could bring to bear on their recovery journey including qualities like resilience and self-efficacy, and capacities like positive communication skills

2. **social recovery capital:** which is the sum of the positive supports and resources that the person has access to but is limited by the extent of the person's commitment to that social support network

3. **community recovery capital:** which is the resources available in the community including the quality of treatment supports, the availability and attractiveness of recovery champions and the availability of reasonable housing and jobs in the area

A further analysis of the effect of recovery capital comes from a PhD study reported in a book chapter by Landale and Best (2012). This is a study based on a group of young, recidivistic offenders who were offered the opportunity to engage in a project, Second Chance, which diverted them from the criminal justice system into meaningful activities. To be eligible for the programme, participants had to have been arrested on a minimum of three occasions in the previous year, tested positive (on arrest) for heroin or crack cocaine, and to have failed to engage in treatment. While not all of those who engaged in the programme showed significant improvements, those who did were characterised by changes in personal, social and community capital. Based on a model developed by Dingle *et al* (2011) of the impact of engagement in meaningful activities, the model that is most effective in explaining this change is of a snowballing dynamic of change:

- Participation in the football team that was at the centre of the Second Chance programme improved emotion regulation and generated a sense of accomplishment challenging the assumption that the individual was caught in a cycle of hopelessness and intoxication.

- This in turn generated and was prompted by changes in their social networks away from the socially excluded groups of fellow users and offenders to include the coaches, other members of the team and opponents. In other words, participation created the opportunity for the widening of the social network and the development of new networks who were either aspiring to recovery or who were unrelated to the drug scene.

- And this is the final key component of change, which is access to social capital. Based on the ideas outlined by Putnam (2000) about social capital, access to social support is also access to information and opportunity. Community capital in this sense is both the likelihood of finding out about opportunities that arise (houses, courses, jobs) in the community and also the sense that they are available and accessible to you.

The Second Chance project demonstrated that actively encouraging engagement in meaningful activities creates not only a sense of well-being but also access to a new social network and new social support systems. This is important through the doors it opens to the resources that exist in the community, something particularly important for people whose social networks consist almost exclusively of those who are socially marginalised and excluded. We will return to this theme of social and community capital in the following chapter.

This work also developed a collaboration with two eminent recovery academics – William White, a leading international recovery expert, and Teodora Groshkova, a research academic who has worked at the Institute of Psychiatry in London and the European Monitoring Centre for Drugs and Drug Addiction (EMCDDA) in Lisbon. Our collaboration has yielded two instruments that are used in the study of recovery in professionals.

Initially, we amended a checklist that William White had developed of recovery community participation into a coherent research scale – the Recovery Group Participation Scale (RGPS; Groshkova *et al,* 2011). This is a 14-item measure that assesses engagement in a range of mutual aid recovery groups and commitment to the recovery group process. This was a deliberate attempt to move away from the existing measures of mutual aid involvement, which typically focused on Alcoholics Anonymous, thereby allowing individuals to include a much wider array of recovery groups in their communities.

The same research partnership then worked on developing a measure of recovery capital – starting with a series of workshops with the Lothians and Edinburgh Abstinence Project (LEAP) whose clients helped us identify the most appropriate domains for the instrument. In the initial version, still used in some locations, there were 100 items – 50 of recovery strengths and 50 of recovery 'threats' or weaknesses. However, the version that was tested for reliability and validity (Groshkova *et al*, 2012) and subsequently published was the 50-item scale based only on recovery strengths or resources. In this assessment, participants simply endorse by ticking the items they agree with and leave blank the remainder. The scale splits into two sub-scales of 25 items each measuring personal recovery capital and social recovery capital and each of these sub-scales in turn consists of five domain scales of five items. The underlying idea is that recovery capital is a form of 'currency' for recovery – a fluid and dynamic currency that will shift with changes in circumstances, social networks and life events, but that provides a mechanism for measuring the supports and resources a person has at their disposal.

These two scales (Recovery Group Participation Scale and Assessment of Recovery Capital) are both included in the current study as measures of key components of recovery – personal recovery capital, social recovery capital and community recovery engagement. However, the aim of the study was to assess well-being and functioning using these measures of recovery capital as well as the WHO Brief Quality of Life scale (Skevington *et al*, 2004), and an assessment of physical and psychological health (drawn from the Maudsley Addiction Profile, Marsden *et al*, 1998).

The second type of analysis collected in the current project is a biographical account of events and reports in the recovery journey. There is a long tradition of the 'timeline followback' as a method of collecting historical data by providing dates and markers to cue recollection of key life events, and for the current study, I used the Lifetime Drug Use History that I had developed with colleagues in Birmingham (Best *et al*, 2008a, 2008b; Day *et al*, 2008). This provided not only a quantitative frame for the biographical accounts of recovery, it also provided an event-based approach to prepare the participant for the qualitative exploration of the key events in their recovery journey.

Piloting this method in Australia

I was working as Head of Research and Workforce Development at Turning Point Alcohol and Drug Centre in Melbourne for the period of data collection for the current stories. In this time, the focus of the organisation switched from primarily focused on harm reduction to an increasing interest in recovery and the transmission of messages of hope to all kinds of clients engaged with Turning Point services. This coincided with a recognition of the emergence of recovery as an organising concept for treatment services and systems that met with and provoked considerable opposition from some quarters (Anex, 2012; AIVL, 2012). At the time of writing, the recovery approach has had a significant impact on policy at a state level in Victoria but has continued to be viewed with considerable suspicion and mistrust in both treatment and especially addiction academic contexts.

To provide further context, Turning Point is unusual in that a substantial proportion of its clinical services are provided in the telephone and online space with 24-hour counselling provided by email and by telephone, primarily for Victoria but with some services (particularly for gambling) that covered all of Australia. The Turning Point website offers a major opportunity for raising awareness of recovery to a much wider range of people – professionals, family members as well as individuals at all stages of their own recovery journeys – than would typically be exposed to recovery stories and messages. The organisation agreed, in mid-2013, to start collating recovery stories that could be summarised and edited for inclusion on the Turning Point website, as a prelude to the development of a webpage on the site devoted exclusively to recovery stories, and the data that are presented in Chapter 3 are part of that initial data collection process.

With assistance from the primary user and carer involvement group – the Eastern Health Consumer and Carer Advisory Council – a brief rationale and research instrument based on the six phases of the recovery journey – were developed and piloted. An initial cluster of 50 stories were collected in this way through a combination of recovery group meeting attendance, word of mouth and active recruitment by a small number of peers, and these are described in some depth in the previous chapter. This component is crucial to the project as its aim was to characterise the experiences of individuals in recovery – and many of the same biographical and narrative questions have been used in the current study. The rationale for this is simple – to provide a basic context of well-being and functioning, to create a biographical review and to explore (using more open and qualitative techniques) the stages and turning points of the recovery journey.

Design and method for the recovery stories of professionals

This basic developmental sequence is then supplemented by an assessment of current functioning and an attempt to make sense of the experience of visibility. The initial phase of the interview is a structured questionnaire that can be researcher-administered or self-completed depending on the preference of the participant and the practicalities of the context. In terms of structured measures that have been used in the study, **table 5.1** provides an overview of the instruments that have been employed in the current study.

Table 5.1: Key measures used in the current study		
Instrument	Key properties	Use in the current analysis
Maudsley Addiction Profile (Marsden *et al*, 1998) physical and psychological health sections	Established outcome indicator providing brief with established psychometric credentials (20 items)	To provide a current assessment of physical and psychological functioning
WHO-Bref Quality of Life Scale (Skevington *et al*, 2008)	Established measure of four components of quality of life – physical, psychological, social and environmental (26 items)	To provide data on well-being that can be compared against population norms
Recovery Group Participation Scale (Groshkova *et al*, 2011)	Measure of engagement in range of recovery groups (14 items)	To provide a basic measure of ongoing recovery group involvement and activity
Assessment of Recovery Capital (Groshkova *et al*, 2012)	Measure of personal and social recovery capital (50 items)	To provide an assessment of areas of strength in recovery and the balance between personal and social recovery capital
Lifetime Drug Use History (Best *et al*, 2008a; Day *et al*, 2008)	In-depth grid of substance use history and timeline follow-back method to assess substance use sequences and patterns across the life course	To provide a developmental pathway and map of recovery experiences and journeys
Recovery narrative (Best *et al*, 2011b)	Based on the Glasgow Recovery Study, this is a series of open-ended questions asking about experiences of stages of the recovery journey	To provide a personalised account of the addiction and recovery journey

This fits into a structure and rationale that is essentially in three phases:

1. a personal account of the recovery journey
2. a life chart (timeline follow-back) denoting key events in the recovery journey
3. a measure of current functioning.

The qualitative component is as outlined above:

1. The experience of acute addiction – why substance use started, how it escalated and why it became problematic
2. Initial attempts at stopping and their effects – this section aims to encourage participants to reflect on initial and unsuccessful quit attempts
3. Final and successful cessation attempt – in contrast, they are then encouraged to reflect in more detail on the final and successful cessation attempt
4. Early stages of recovery and transition to a recovery lifestyle – participants are encouraged to discuss how life changed over the course of the early recovery years
5. Stable recovery – how long they consider they have been in stable recovery for and what this transition felt like
6. Life as it currently is

Additionally, participants were asked two further questions:

1. What do you think of the recovery movement in the UK or Australia?
2. How open have you been about your recovery status professionally, and what impact has this had on your career?

The aim was to recruit roughly equal groups of addiction professionals in Australia and the UK to participate in the study – the target sample size was 50 – to provide an understanding of the experiences of recovery in each setting and to embed this within a model of recovery visibility and the benefits and costs of being a visible recovery champion while working as a professional in the alcohol and drug field.

Each of the three following chapters will describe the findings from each of these components and Chapter 9 will attempt to draw together some common themes across the different types of data. These stories are incredibly rich and varied and I cannot do sufficient credit to the sense of inspiration and hope that emanates from these stories of life transformation.

References

Anex (2012) *Australian Drug Policy: Harm reduction and new recovery: Discussion paper*. Melbourne, Australia: Anex.

Australian Injecting and Illicit Drug Users' League (AIVL) (2012) *'New Recovery', Harm Reduction and Drug Use Policy Statement*. Melbourne, Australia: AIVL.

Best D, Day E, Cantillano V, Gaston R, Nambamali A, Sweeting R & Keaney F (2008a) Mapping heroin careers: utilising a standardized history-taking method to assess the speed of escalation of heroin using careers in a treatment-seeking cohort. *Drug and Alcohol Review* **27** 169–174.

Best D, Ghufran S, Day E, Ray R & Loaring J (2008b) Breaking the habit: A retrospective analysis of desistance factors among formerly problematic heroin users. *Drug and Alcohol Review* **27** 619–624.

Best D & Laudet A (2010) *The Potential of Recovery Capital*. RSA Projects. London: Royal Society for the Arts.

Best D, Gow T, Taylor A, Knox A & White W (2011a) Recovery from heroin or alcohol dependence: a qualitative account of the recovery experience in Glasgow. *Journal of Drug Issues* **11** (1) 359–378.

Best D, Gow J, Taylor A, Knox T, Groshkova T & White W (2011b) Mapping the recovery stories of drinkers and drug users in Glasgow: quality of life and its associations with measures of recovery capital. *Drug and Alcohol Review* **31** (3) 334–341.

Best D (2012) *Addiction Recovery: A movement for personal change and social growth in the UK*. Brighton: Pavilion.

Day E, Best D, Cantillano V, Gaston V, Nambamali A & Keaney F (2008) Measuring the use and career histories of drug users in treatment: Reliability of the Lifetime Drug Use History (LDUH) and its data yield relative to clinical case notes. *Drug and Alcohol Review* **27** 175–181.

Dingle G *et al* (2012) 'To be heard': the social and mental health benefits of choir singing for disadvantaged adults. *Psychology of Music* doi: 10.1177/0305735611430081.

Granfield R & Cloud W (2001) Social context and natural recovery: The role of social capital in overcoming drug-associated problems. *Substance Use and Misuse* **36** 1543–1570.

Groshkova T, Best D & White W (2011) Recovery Group Participation Scale (RGPS): factor structure in alcohol and heroin recovery populations. *Journal of Groups in Addiction and Recovery* **6** 76–92.

Groshkova T, Best D & White W (2012) The Assessment of Recovery Capital: Properties and psychometrics of a measure of addiction recovery strengths. *Drug and Alcohol Review* **32** (2) 187–194.

HM Government (2010) *Drug Strategy 2010: Reducing demand, restricting supply, building recovery: Supporting people to live a drug-free life*. London: DH.

Hser Y, Longshore D & Anglin M (2007) The life course perspective on drug use: a conceptual framework for understanding drug use. *Trajectories Evaluation Review* **31** 515–547.

Landale S & Best D (2012) Dynamic shifts in social networks and normative values in recovery from an offending and drug using lifestyle (p219-236). In: CD Johnston (ed) *Social Capital: Theory, Measurement and Outcomes*. New York: Nova Science Publishers Inc.

Longabaugh R, Wirtz P, Zyuviak W & O'Malley S (2010), Network support as a prognostive indiciator of drinking outcomes: the COMBINE study. *Journal of Studies on Alcohol and Drugs* **71** 837–846.

Marsden J, Gossop M, Stewart D, Best D, Farrell M, Lehmann P, Edwards C & Strang J (1998) the Maudsley Addiction Profile (MAP): a brief instrument for assessing treatment outcome. *Addiction* **93** (12) 1857–1868.

Phillips L & Shaw A (2013) Substance use more stigmatised than smoking and obesity. *Journal of Substance Use* **18** (4) 247–253.

Putnam R (2000) *Bowling Alone: The collapse and revival of American community*. New York: Simon and Schuster.

Skevington S, Lotfy M & O'Connell K (2004) The World Health Organization's WHOQOL-BREF quality of life assessment: psychometric properties and results of the international field trial. A report from the WHOQOL group. *Quality of Life Research* **13** 299–310.

Chapter 6: Case studies of recovery stories

An introduction and reflection on participation

This chapter presents recovery stories from addiction professionals in the form of vignettes illustrated with quotations where appropriate. As the addictions treatment field is small in both the UK and Australia, names and details have been changed to protect the anonymity of participants. The stories outlined in this, and the following two chapters are incredibly rich in their detail and strengths and are testimony to the honesty and bravery of those who provided them, as well as incredible human accomplishments in overcoming adversity.

They are also unusual as research stories in that I know personally many of those (although by no means all) who have contributed their stories. Indeed, I have utilised personal networks and made great demands of friendship to have these stories told and I owe a considerable debt of gratitude to participants in this project who have given their time and have laid themselves bare in providing these very personal life and recovery histories. So I am sensitised to the need to protect the identities of the individuals whose stories are laid out, particularly in this chapter, where I use personal narratives to tell the stories of recovery. I have changed some biographical details and all of the names to attempt to preserve some anonymity and I apologise to those whose stories feel too distorted – I have tried to retain as much of the spirit of the story without allowing a guessing game where those in the field will be able to identify their colleagues and friends.

These stories have also been collected in both Australia and the UK – and nowhere else. And there is a reason for this. While the advent of a recovery model elicited resistance from a number of groups (in particular the vested interests of the medical fraternity), and some understandable anxieties with the perceived links to 'payment by results' under the coalition government in the UK (summarised in Ashton's article *The New Abstentionists*; Ashton, 2008), these have been relatively mild in comparison to the active hostility in Australia (AIVL, 2012; Anex, 2012). In my early recovery presentations, a number of people would speak to me about how they were reluctant to report their recovery status for fear of adverse effects on their careers. This fear is entirely justified as Australia contains a small but vociferous core of harm reduction activists (a coalition of primary care physicians, university-based academics and user group representatives, as well as a number of professionals in the field) who have actively attempted to suppress discussion about recovery in Australia.

Indeed, one eminent Australian harm reduction activist tried to prevent me from speaking to medical students about recovery while another circulated a message to his colleagues in the Australasian Chapter of Addiction Medicine suggesting that recovery was 'dangerous' and should not be encouraged. It is in this context that a comparison of Australian and UK recovery experiences is particularly important. In Australia, 'recovery' is seen by many professionals as the antithesis of 'harm reduction' and is associated with right-wing politics, with the mutual aid movement and with anxieties about reductions in funding for treatment and support services.

The salience of visibility

The model of recovery I have developed is fundamentally a developmental and ecological model – people grow into recovery but they do so based on the opportunities for recovery available in the community they live in. The most critical part of this community is the accessibility, visibility and attractiveness of recovery. If there are no role models of recovery that are available, or those that are available offer neither the hope that recovery is a realistic goal nor that it is something attractive or worth aspiring to, then recovery is significantly less likely. So there are two questions that are particularly important to this population of people in recovery who are workers in the alcohol and drug field – the first is around their experience of being supported in their recovery journeys and the second is about their own role as 'recovery champions' (HM Government, 2010) who act as the inspiration and motivation for role modelling – and the extent to which people in recovery embrace the idea of being a 'role model' for the social learning of recovery (Moos, 2007).

Underlying this model is the idea that recovery is a social contagion. Based on the ideas that Christakis and Fowler (2010) developed in their work on the Framingham Heart Study, behaviour change is characterised as something that is socially transmitted via group involvement and modelling of behaviour. The Framingham effects around the transmission of obesity, of binge drinking, of smoking cessation and of divorce all point to the idea that a diverse range of behaviours spread through social networks on the basis of connection (who is linked to whom), contagion (what it is that flows across links) and homophily (the idea that people who spend time together have common values and beliefs). The latter approach is entirely consistent with the social identity model advanced by Jetten *et al* (2011) in that it is the incorporation of group norms and values that is seen to underpin the behavioural component of social identity and its impact on behaviour. The key underlying idea is that recovery spreads through social processes, both interpersonal and through group processes and norms.

The extrapolation of this work is that recovery spreads in groups through similar processes. For recovery to spread in groups, it is necessary for connection to be established between people aspiring to recovery and those who are already engaged in this behaviour. Second, it requires that the recovery behaviours of the existing 'champions' are transmitted – this is the principle of contagion. Third, that those early in or aspiring to recovery come to adopt the same beliefs and values as those in recovery and so homophily binds to the group but also to the behaviours and attitudes the recovery groups and champions model and promote. For this process to work there have to be bridges that can link those in early recovery with mentors or champions who can model recovery values and behaviours, and whose role modelling is sufficiently strong to promote effective contagion and incorporation of those values and practices.

This is exemplified in the UK Drug Strategy (HM Government, 2010) which talks of three levels of 'recovery champions' – strategic, therapeutic and community. These are the people who actively celebrate and promote recovery – and who are visible transmitters of the five elements of the CHIME model (Leamy *et al,* 2011) from mental health research. Recovery champions support and enable recovery by embodying Connectedness, Hope, Identity, Meaning and Empowerment, and successfully role modelling it to the point of imitation and through the establishment of recovery values in groups. They are the people who enable recovery to be perceived as visible, accessible and attractive by those in active addiction or who are struggling to maintain their own recovery. For the current sample, the critical question is around barriers to becoming a visible recovery champion and what happens to individuals who are overt in the workplace.

The work on the development of recovery-oriented systems of care from the US (Centre for Substance Abuse Treatment, 2009) speaks extensively of recovery awareness and positive recovery practices in the professional AOD workforce, and also speaks about peer organisations but offers almost no support and guidance around the role of people in recovery who are in the professional workforce. There are two component parts to this – one relates to stigma and the other to active engagement in recovery communities. If people in recovery are open with their colleagues about their recovery status, then they may be subject to being treated as 'different' particularly in the more acute, clinically-oriented services – and if the service does not have a strong recovery orientation. Second, there is the communication of recovery status to clients and its potential impact on the professional relationships of worker and counsellor.

Additionally, an issue arises around the linkage between recovery champions and the strength that can be derived from collective recovery engagement, not only through mutual aid groups but through the emerging peer recovery movement, something that has become increasingly prominent in both the UK and Australia in recent years. The strongest action research example of this I have seen is through the recovery community work I was involved in in the South Yorkshire mining town of Barnsley (Best *et al,* 2013). I was asked to plan and run a series of seminars in Barnsley, primarily targeting specialist addiction treatment staff but also to be available to partner agencies and the community recovery groups already in existence in Barnsley. Around 80 people attended the sessions which closed with asking people to sign up to become local recovery champions, to promote and engage in recovery support activities in Barnsley. This in turn led to around 35 individuals signing up of whom around 15–20 went on to form the core membership of the Barnsley Recovery Coalition. This group initiated a series of activities – a float in the annual Lord Mayor's parade, a recovery walk, a recovery fun day and an art walk – that created a sense of vibrancy around recovery. They created a visible and active recovery community that engaged in positive activities and personified the CHIME model of recovery. Their activities and their coalescence into a positive group was at the centre of the emergence of an attractive, visible and accessible recovery community for Barnsley.

The key point of this is that recovery activity in an area can become contagious through initiatives such as the one described in Barnsley or in a much more personal and idiosyncratic way, that relies on individual champions. One of the purposes of the case studies – and of the book as a whole – is to characterise what it means to be a recovery champion. Therefore, the scale of recovery group participation will allow examination of the ongoing engagement in recovery communities and what relationship this has to being active as a recovery champion.

Introducing the case studies

There are six recovery stories presented below – the first three from the UK and the next three from Australia. They are all important stories in their own right, transmitting hope and incredible personal achievement – but they have been selected to demonstrate the key aspects of the dynamic model of developmental recovery capital. What is presented in this chapter is a summary of the personal experiences and stories of individual recovery as a life-course developmental process, the current situation of the individual in terms of quality of life and well-being, and their experiences of discrimination and its impact on their role as a recovery champion.

Kitty's story

Kitty is an active recovery champion who is highly visible and has been responsible for driving a recovery community in her hometown and other areas of Northern Ireland. She has been extremely open about her own recovery experiences and is active in a range of mutual aid recovery groups. Her history involves three substances – alcohol, cannabis and cocaine – but with alcohol as the dominant part of her addiction and recovery experience. Although currently working in the alcohol and drug field as a community development worker and inspirational speaker, she did not do so while an active addict, and her social identity is embedded within a recovery world and her active role as a recovery advocate and champion.

She is divorced and lives with her sons and part of her recovery journey was about getting her children back out of care, and the reinstatement of family was both a strong motive for initiating recovery, but also represented the kind of social recovery capital that has sustained and enabled the development of stable recovery and the resilience and personal resources required for this.

In terms of her substance-using history, like many people, drinking started at school age, and illicit drug use when she was a law student. Daily drinking and drug use started at 18, and she estimates that alcohol dependence also started at this age. This continued largely unbroken for 17 years with only one brief period of abstinence, and she describes the escalation as *'it progressed, culminating in losing everything including my children, career, house, job and driving license'*. However, Kitty would also regard her alcohol history as bound up with family and culture – a heavy drinking cultural heritage and immediate family drinking culture, and a history of alcohol problems in the family.

In her own narrative, the damage was also seen as cumulative and progressive, *'I was tired of the consequences. It was costing me more than the drink. I had had enough and I wanted to change'*. Her key turning point was an arrest for drunk driving at the age of 35 which resulted in her losing custody of her child.

This also prompted AA engagement – not for the first time as there had been earlier episodes at 24 and 33, but this was the first sustained engagement, which continued for the eight years up to the interview point. This is indicative of the idea that recovery progress is not linear and that the recognition of a problem will not automatically prompt lasting change. It is also important to note that engagement with AA (or other mutual aid groups) is not always immediately successful, and individuals may have to be ready to embrace the values and roles needed for recovery.

For Kitty, AA was also responsible for a spiritual experience at the age of 38 – one of two key recovery points described – the other being the engagement with an AA group overseas. The initial stages of the recovery journey were experienced as hard, '*Year one was hideous! I had a lot going on … trying to regain custody of my children, finding work, trying to build relationships with my family and staying abstinent by really becoming a member of AA*'. For Kitty, as for many people in recovery, the journey is not just about stopping using, but about rebuilding a life with a different set of goals and values and about finding the solutions to stopping using and to building a life that is meaningful and satisfying.

In terms of current well-being and functioning, hers is a story of success with almost no residual physical or psychological distress and exceptionally high scores for personal and social recovery capital and for quality of life. She also scores 13/14 on recovery group participation, indicative of an incredibly strong immersion in active recovery group activity and participation. Hers is a recovery story that involves no formal treatment but an incredible commitment to community recovery both in terms of mutual aid and active participation in the recovery movement. Kitty is only around five years into her recovery journey and it remains a highly salient social identity for her (Jetten *et al*, 2009) – while for other people, non-addict identities that do not involve recovery will become more salient early in the recovery story. She is highly respected in both her professional roles and is widely recognised as a major recovery champion for Northern Ireland.

Kitty's story is important in illustrating a couple of major issues about recovery – the first is that it does not necessarily involve treatment and so, using the language of Granfield and Cloud (1996), Kitty's is an example of 'natural recovery'. Second, although AA played a prominent part in her recovery journey, it was only on the third attempt and on finding the right group, that Kitty was able to make a lasting change in her recovery journey. Thus, recovery should not be seen as a linear process but as one in which change is event-triggered (turning points) but predicated on both individual developmental process and on the environmental supports and contextual factors that enable recovery to be sustained. The developmental model as outlined in Best (2012) is that individuals have to have sufficient recovery capital (and I would now amend that to say that this is primarily social capital) to allow them to maximise windows of opportunity for change.

For Kitty, the recovery journey is one of social learning and social control embedded within the 12-step movement where both sponsors and the group have played a powerful role in supporting her to develop a recovery identity, that is salient and sustained through her role as a recovery champion and a 'recovery ambassador'. She has incredibly high recovery capital and is immersed in a developmental pathway that is visible and positive and her negative experiences of disclosure of recovery status are restricted to her previous role in another profession. This is a story in which recovery identity becomes incredibly powerful and a dominant personal and social identity.

Sally's story

The second story is also taken from the UK and is the recovery story of a senior addictions service manager working in the AOD field.

Sally is a 44-year old female living in the north of England who has a level of residual physical health problems and some ongoing issues with anxiety. Nonetheless her general quality of life is good and she reports extremely high recovery capital scoring 48/50 on the Assessment of Recovery Capital (including 25/25 for personal recovery capital). She regards herself as having completed her recovery journey, '*I am grateful that I regard myself as recovered rather than as being in recovery as this has enabled me to evolve a new career trajectory as the director of a treatment service for people with addiction*'. For Sally, recovery is much more of a personal than a social identity as recovery is not seen by her as membership of a community but a personal lived status that is only shared in an abstract sense, and the act of sharing is not regarded as an intrinsic part of her recovery journey.

Sally started drinking seriously as a student, '*I binge drank as a student without too much concern or negative consequences*' but moving into a second professional post meant that she was drinking daily, such that '*the regular transposed into the habitual quite quickly as I have always had addictive traits and suddenly I became aware I was in full blown dependency*'. The individuality of recovery pathways is also reflected in the individuality of addiction careers – for Sally, daily and dependent drinking did not start until around 36 and drinking peaked at the age of 37. The peak period of drinking was also associated with the decision to stop and to initiate the recovery journey, and there was a relatively short gap between the two.

For Sally, there was a trigger then a gradual shift to change. *'I decided to stop drinking after reassessing my life following [a personal life tragedy involving a death in the family] … in the year following her death, I tried to stop several times without success. This led to me lying to friends and family and hiding my drinking which actually escalated due to panic'*. In total, she attempted to stop three times without success. *'It felt as though I needed to change everything and completely start again to have any chance of making recovery a reality'*. Her route to recovery involved two salient components – the first a physical relocation and the second a complete change of profession and career pathway to a job that involved setting up her own addiction treatment consultancy business and committing a large number of hours to working. In developmental terms, the removal of social networks and cues for substance use is consistent with the findings of Longabaugh *et al* (2010) and Best *et al* (2008) that changes in social supports are an essential part of the transition to recovery and these are generally associated with changes in routines and practices.

'Once I had established a new pattern of living in the first year, I started to be rewarded with a better quality of life which in itself became something to nurture and cherish… As each year has passed, I have moved further away from feeling like an addict although I choose to honour my addictive past by considering myself a recovered addict, as I have learned much from my journey and don't regret what being an alcoholic has taught me about life and how we manage our feelings and the situations we encounter'. This is where the notion of 'recovery spin' can be identified (Ronel & Elisha, 2011) in that the transition to recovery elicits the perception of improved life quality, which in turn enables and sustains further recovery growth and the development of greater recovery capital.

In terms of treatment engagement, there are two key experiences – the first is regular contact with a clinical psychologist and the second attendance at AA. These two things coincided and were initiated around one year before achieving enduring abstinence and both continued for another two years. They also coincided with the decision to take a change in career path. In her account of her recovery journey, therapy is afforded much more prominence than AA – *'with the help of [eminent psychologist], I explored my life, feelings, coping strategies and ambitions and realised that alcohol was exacerbating my difficulties rather than alleviating anything'* – interestingly, AA does not merit a mention in this account of change in spite of attendance going on for more than two years. And this is critical to the idea that the pathways to recovery are both complex and personal – and that while for many people, 12-step groups may be at the centre of their recovery journey, for others they will play no role. It is, however, relatively unusual for mutual aid to play a peripheral role as appears to be the case in Sally's story. Sally's story is also unusual in that there is a significant continuing role for an addiction professional and so her recovery involves a continuing engagement with professional support that has outlasted mutual aid and peer support.

Sally's recovery story is unusual in its assertion that the recovery journey is now complete and can be commemorated as such, and that this sense of completion is seen as a source of strength, although therapy remains a central aspect of her life. The transformation to recovery is therefore characterised as a kind of rebirth in which a physical relocation is linked to a career change and to becoming an addiction professional as a key staging post in the transition from addict to ex-addict. The addiction career is also unusual in that it starts late and is of relatively short duration, with alcohol use in late adolescence being described as under control. In Sally's case, addiction and recovery is linked to a major life event (and so turning point) in the form of a personal tragedy, and so recovery is intrinsically caught up with grief and the struggle to move forward. With Sally, there is also a huge emphasis on work as something that filled time in early recovery and became a major part of the transition to a new identity and value system that excluded alcohol. It is the story of a strong and committed woman who characterises addiction as a developmental process and part of a process of becoming – in some ways what would more accurately be referred to as 'eudaimonia' (human flourishing) than recovery. There is another quality of eudaimonia that is relevant to this case study – that sense of giving back as part of living a just and worthwhile life.

The discussion of the merits of the word 'recovery' in the previous chapter is I think best illustrated in the case of Sally where she both regards herself as having 'recovered' in the existing dichotomy but that the ex-addict identity has not been completely shed. In other words, while addiction is no longer an active part of her current identity it is a part of the developmental trajectory and the related narrative for the person she currently is. It is a pathway of growth and learning and development that had led her to the insights and strengths and values she currently possesses. This is a much more useful conceptualisation (which, as will be illustrated below, is not contingent on seeing oneself as recovered) than a recovery concept which has implications of going back. There is a second important ramification which is around the idea of transition from an excluded group to the normal strivings and endeavours of everyday life – the recognition that recovery life is not perfect but that the recovery journey provides the individual with a unique set of skills and capabilities for facing the challenges all of us face.

It is also interesting that in Sally's case, recovery does not involve any ongoing participation in recovery groups or communities, and that this is fundamental to the notion of being 'recovered' yet there is still a component of 'giving back' by working in the alcohol and drug field. Sally generally does not disclose her recovery status to clients as *'the focus of my work is around their stories not mine'* but will do so if she feels it is in the best interests of the client. In contrast she reports that *'I am very open, however, with my peers and colleagues and in other professional circles'* and she felt that this had resulted in no negative effects or experiences. Her involvement in the recovery movement is inspired by this desire to support and help others – *'I hope that by classifying myself as an ex-addict and being more visible as a professional with an addiction history I will enable others to recognise their reliance on substances and feel able to access support they can identify with'*.

Thus the recovery identity is an important part of Sally's current identity through her role modelling of recovery hope through the transmission of hope and by creating a visible link where it is needed for people struggling with addiction issues.

Graham's story

Graham is a 38-year old man living in the south of England who reported that he had been in recovery for 14 years from an addiction history that combined alcohol, heroin, cocaine and benzodiazepines. He works as a recovery co-ordinator for a major UK specialist addiction treatment provider and so recovery is embedded within his professional role.

Unusually, heroin use preceded problem drinking in Graham's story, commencing heroin use at the age of 15 and becoming dependent at 18. He cycled through a number of community and residential treatment episodes between the ages of 20 and 24 (including three residential detoxifications and four periods of residential rehabilitation) before becoming actively involved in Narcotics' Anonymous at 25 (and this involvement continuing for the 13 years up to the time of the interview). The cumulative weariness of the lifestyle was cited as the motive for finally stopping and he describes this as being *'physically, emotionally and spiritually bankrupt'* along with a *'feeling of utter desolation, loneliness and pain'*.

In developmental terms he described the first year of his recovery journey as being safe in a treatment centre and '*I would not have wanted to be anywhere else in the world*', although he reported that he was extremely anxious and fearful for the first two months. Once the first year was complete, and he left treatment, there were some painful challenges but he reported that each year got better, and from this point '*using was no longer an option*' although '*relationships with family and sexual relationships were challenging and something that required ongoing therapy*'. Graham is a good example of someone who continues with a twin track of continuing an overt recovery journey through active participation in recovery groups and communities but who is also addressing those wider issues around relationships and careers and personal growth.

He scored 11/14 on the Recovery Group Participation Scale indicating considerable ongoing immersion in the recovery community and his social network contained more than 100 other people in recovery, indicating both high recovery visibility and a strong recovery social identity. In spite of this he is not immediately open about his recovery status in work. '*At work where it could be of such massive benefit, I have more reluctance*', which he attributes to the fact that the '*treatment field does not respect, understand or value the position of the recovering alcoholic or addict. When I first came into the addiction field I was naïvely open about this and have regretted it in some quarters since*'. He goes on to say that, '*I feel that the majority of the treatment field is interested in prescribing as this is where the money is.*'

This is driven in part by a scepticism around the recovery movement in the UK. '*Unfortunately the term "recovery" has been co-opted in an industry that is now driven by statistics*' leading to a lowering of the bar and a loss of standards in the recovery movement. This is linked to what he perceives is a neglect of the 12-step movement in current UK treatment models. '*I find it sad that at a time when money for the addiction field is at an all-time low, especially for abstinence-based recovery, there is such resistance towards the 12-step models that have helped so many people. The vast majority of addicts and alcoholics working in the field have achieved their recovery through this model*'. There is a clear disjunction between his role as a 'recovery co-ordinator' in a professional context and his own beliefs about the recovery movement and its effectiveness.

Graham's addiction career had an early onset with the initiation of heroin injecting at 18 and a heroin-using career that escalated to two grams per day by the age of 23. Additionally, he was a heavy user of diazepam, alcohol and cocaine, and was homeless at the age of 19. His pathway to recovery involved multiple episodes of residential detoxification and rehabilitation, but it was engagement with 12-step at the age of 25 that initiated a recovery journey that had continued (with ongoing NA involvement) for 13 years. The 'recovery spin' for Graham involved fathering two children and becoming involved in the addiction field, although the disclosure of recovery status has come at a cost for Graham and he is sceptical about the 'recovery movement' and its impact on UK policy.

Glenn's story

The first of the three Australian recovery stories was provided by Glenn, a 51-year-old senior clinician who is not in an overtly recovery-focused role, but is based in a service with a strong recovery focus. Glenn is unusual in that he categorised himself as being both in recovery and recovered and has been abstinent from all psychoactive substances for more than 25 years.

Although he started drinking at the age of 12, his primary problem with heroin, starting with using and injecting at the age of 17, and initiating daily use by 19. His substance-using career also involved cocaine and cannabis. He was dependent on heroin from the age of 18 to the age of 30. For him prison was the motive for stopping. '*I decided I had done enough prison – but I only wanted to stop heroin, I still wanted to drink and use pot. I learnt about addiction and how it impacted on my drug use decisions – that was about six months into treatment*'. Recovery was initiated following a period of residential treatment that was then followed by active engagement in Narcotics Anonymous, and starting work in the alcohol and drug field. Mutual aid attendance continued for around four years, and this ended around the time he got married and then purchased his first house. However, for Glenn, the early stage of recovery was about learning a new way to live, '*I began to experience (or taste) life in a different way, no drive to use, no crime, no police, no violence. I had a job and was able to enjoy life*'.

The experiential component of this journey was that he '*got bailed to rehab and began to learn it was more than simply drug use – this gave me something to work with other than just not using. Also seeing people I knew from the streets or prison who seemed to be doing OK*'. In terms of the CHIME model (Leamy *et al*, 2011), this is the emergence of hope and its combination with identification with individuals already in recovery who inspire the belief that recovery is possible. This creates the possibility for social learning and incorporation of recovery values and practices and the initiation of a meaningful recovery identity.

Glenn describes his life now as '*something that requires maintenance, there are things to do, responsibilities to accept, status in the community, a good recreational and social life, and I have achieved some of the luxuries of life. My family – wife and children – are important and enjoyable'*. Glenn's journey is embedded within the TC recovery model where addiction is not seen as ongoing and where he now lives life as an ex-addict, and he points out that *'I am not defined by who I used to be'*. Nonetheless, he has a strong commitment to the recovery movement both through his work and a personal commitment to recovery. He concluded the interview with the statement that *'whether a person stays connected for the rest of their life or whether they use the recovery movement as a springboard back into mainstream society, it is critical that the recovery movement is there for people to gain the support they need to effect the changes they need to make, particularly early in recovery'*.

Glenn is a person who has achieved long-term recovery following an extensive poly-substance using career which resulted in considerable criminal justice involvement. His recovery was a result of engagement in both therapeutic community and 12-step treatment, that created the foundations for a positive 'recovery spin' in which strong social capital was developed in the form of marriage and employment, and subsequently the birth of children and the purchase of a house. For Glenn, the definition of recovery is about quality of life and his experience of recovery is a long-term transition from low to high recovery capital based on family and a sense of purpose and positive identity. One interesting footnote to Glenn's story as a recovered person is that he is very clear that this is something that he does not disclose to neighbours and its role is exclusively within the workplace. He will disclose it if will help people in early recovery, but not outside the work context where his concerns are around stigma and discrimination.

Anna's story

Anna is a 41-year old woman who lives in Sydney and works as a researcher and part-time clinician in the addictions field. She is in recovery from alcohol problems and is an active member of both AA and Al-Anon and the latter role as an adult child of an alcoholic plays a prominent role in her identity. Her immersion in the mutual aid fellowship is indicated by the fact that she scores 12/14 on the Recovery Group Participation Scale while her social network is composed primarily of people in recovery – almost exactly two-thirds of her social network are other people in recovery.

Her history is of early onset alcohol problems with daily drinking initiated around the age of 16 and heavy drinking peaking in the teenage years. This was compounded by cannabis use starting at 16 and escalating over the teenage years. Her alcohol problems escalated to the point where it resulted in homelessness, which resulted in a hospitalisation following an attack on the streets. This prompted the first of three unsuccessful attempts at cessation of drinking – however, the successful quit attempt was initiated when her ex-partner died and she felt that her life was getting out of control. Around the same time, at the age of 35, she heard an advert for AA on the radio and felt that this was the only possible solution to her problems. This was around 16 years after initiating drinking and around 15 years after her first quit attempt.

While the first year of Anna's recovery is described by her as a 'rollercoaster' that included being *'euphoric about sobriety; plenty of time, money and energy'*, the next three years were *'stabilising but facing issues … was deeply depressed, then got to the point of letting go of old ideas (as part of the AA programme)'* then after starting antidepressants in the third year she reported a significant improvement in how she felt.

At the time of the interview, her current functioning involved some continuing physical and psychological health issues, and she continued with antidepressant medication, and her quality of life and recovery capital were generally positive. Hers is an unusual recovery story in that her father has also been in recovery from alcohol problems for the last five years and this is described as a major factor in Anna's own recovery journey.

For Anna, the death of her partner at 35 was a major turning point, but it was only really the intention to achieve lasting recovery and it took a further two years until the combination of a feeling of being out of control and the opportunity to engage with AA that her recovery became established. This not only evidences the complexity of the initiation of recovery journeys but also the intrinsically dynamic aspect of them. Only through engaging in AA with a subsequent social and public commitment to recovery, that the social identity of recovery becomes established and the opportunities for positive recovery spin to become established. Perhaps serendipitously, the establishment of her recovery has also coincided with her father achieving recovery from alcohol, and it is possible to speculate that there is some element of recovery contagion in this process. This is particularly likely as Anna's social world and social identity is strongly enmeshed in a recovery world and community and this may afford the resources and strengths to enable recovery role-modelling to others in her immediate family context as well as those she engages with in a professional context.

Ken's story

Ken is a 38-year-old male who works as a drug worker with criminal justice clients in Melbourne. He is a committed member of AA and has been involved in service work with the fellowship for a number of years. Ken is long-established in his recovery journey, having achieved abstinence from alcohol 16 years prior to the interview, and having a strong and positive social identity around recovery. In a social network for around 60 people, more than half are also in recovery and this is reflected in a Recovery Group Participation Score of 14/14. Ken is single and his social and work life revolves around his strong commitment to recovery and the social world of recovery.

He started drinking at 13 and by 18 was drinking daily and drinking up to one-and-a-half bottles of spirits per day. This was supplemented with cannabis and between the ages of 18 and 21 he was using around seven grams of cannabis and drinking heavily on a daily basis. Ken had had a history of psychiatric problems and at 21 he first attempted to be admitted to a rehab for alcohol as was worried he was going to have to go back to a psychiatric ward. In total he had around 10 attempts at stopping before he finally managed to stop – and he was driven by *'pain and suffering and by the idea of being permanently in a psychotic state'*.

The first year of his recovery journey he described as *'hell'* although he was very busy with both AA and NA, and things became a bit better between the second and fifth year of his recovery journey when he became *'employable and more stable'* and he attributes his ongoing stability to full-time work and part-time study. In keeping with the philosophy of AA, Ken does not regard his journey as complete and he continues to experience both physical and psychological health symptoms, and reduced quality of life as a result of dissatisfaction with his physical health.

Overall, Ken had a relatively short period of daily substance use (from 18 to 21) but a difficult period of psychiatric problems, suicide attempts and a number of failed attempts at desistance. His recovery was prompted, as is the case in a number of the case studies, by a period of time in rehab followed by active engagement in the mutual aid fellowships, initially both AA and NA but more recently only AA. The period in rehab created the platform for stabilising life enough to allow Ken to participate successfully in AA, and to start the recovery spin of employment and study as well as ongoing participation in 12-step with the resulting emergence of a strong recovery social identity and an accessible recovery support system.

Overview of the case studies

As with a number of the addiction professionals in recovery, onset of problem substance use was early but so also was desistance. In contrast to the arguments advanced by Granfield and Cloud (1996) in their study on natural recovery among middle-class addicts, this population do not appear to have higher personal and social capital during their period of active addiction. However, for many, exit from active addiction is typically relatively early and they typically report relatively short careers of active use. This issue is explored in considerably more detail in the analysis of the Lifetime Drug Use History (LDUH; Day *et al*, 2008) in Chapter 7.

The stories presented earlier are consistent with the developmental model of trigger events that generate a positive recovery spin that results in a positive accrual of personal and social capital and a positive identity that is socially enmeshed. Although the stories differ in the extent to which they characterise recovery as a completed act or an ongoing journey, only in the case of Sally is the ex-addict status associated with no overt social enmeshment in recovery activities, and even in her case, recovery is bound up her vocational choices and her commitment to supporting people to identify and address addiction issues at an earlier stage.

The participants did report mixed experiences and attitudes towards the disclosure of their recovery status with only one person reporting that they had suffered significantly from disclosing recovery status and this had soured his attitudes towards the 'recovery movement' in the UK, largely for lack of authenticity. It is also notable that, while participants can be characterised as coming from either a 12-step or a therapeutic community model, all of the examples cited here have had some engagement with 12-step groups and, for those with TC histories, mutual aid has played an important role in providing continuity from treatment to community recovery. The pathways and developmental processes for the larger recovery group are examined in the next chapter.

References

Anex (2012) *Australian Drug Policy: Harm reduction and new recovery: Discussion paper.* Melbourne, Australia: Anex.

Ashton M (2008) The new abstentionists. *Druglink* Dec/Jan 2008.

Australian Injecting and Illicit Drug Users' League (AIVL) (2012) *New Recovery: Harm reduction and drug use policy statement.* Melbourne, Australia: AIVL.

Best D (2012) *Addiction Recovery: A movement for personal change and social growth in the UK.* Brighton: Pavilion.

Best D, Ghufran S, Day E, Ray R & Loaring J (2008) Breaking the habit: a retrospective analysis of desistance factors among formerly problematic heroin users. *Drug and Alcohol Review* **27** 619–624.

Best D, Loudon L, Powell D, Groshkova T & White W (2013) Identifying and recruiting recovery champions: exploratory action research in Barnsley, South Yorkshire. *Journal of Groups in Addiction and Recovery* **8** (3) 169–184.

Centre for Substance Abuse Treatment (2009) *Guiding Principles and Elements of Recovery-orientated Systems of Care: What do we know from the research Substance Abuse and Mental Health Services Administration.* Rockville, MD: SAMHSA.

Christakis N & Fowler J (2010) *Connected: The amazing power of social networks and how they shape our lives.* London: Harper Press.

Day E, Best D, Cantillano V, Gaston V, Nambamali A & Keaney F (2008) Measuring the use and career histories of drug users in treatment: reliability of the Lifetime Drug Use History (LDUH) and its data yield relative to clinical case notes. *Drug and Alcohol Review* **27** 175–181.

Granfield R & Cloud W (1996) The elephant that nobody sees: Natural recovery among middle class addicts. *Journal of Drug Issues* **26** (1) 45–61.

HM Government (2010) *Drug Strategy 2010: Reducing demand, restricting supply, building recovery: Supporting people to live a drug-free life.* London: DH.

Jetten J, Haslam SA, Iyer A & Haslam C (2009) Turning to others in times of change: Shared identity and coping with stress. In S Stürmer and M Snyder (Eds) *New Directions in the Study of Helping: Group-level perspectives on motivations, consequences and interventions* (pp 139–156). Chichester: Wiley-Blackwell.

Jetten J, Haslam C & Haslam SA (Eds) (2011) *The Social Cure: Identity, health and well-being.* New York: Psychology Press.

Leamy M, Bird V, Le Boutillier C, Williams J & Slade M (2011) Conceptual framework for personal recovery in mental health: systematic review and narrative synthesis. *British Journal of Psychiatry* **199** 445–452.

Longabaugh R, Wirtz P, Zywiak W & O'Malley S (2010) Network support as a prognostic indicator of drinking outcomes: The COMBINE study. *Journal of Studies on Alcohol and Drugs* **71** 837–846.

Moos R (2007) Theory-based active ingredients of effective treatments for substance use disorders. *Drug and Alcohol Dependence* **88** (2–3) 109–121.

Ronel N & Elisha E (2011) A different perspective: introducing positive criminology. *International Journal of Offender Therapy and Comparative Criminology* **2** 305–325.

Chapter 7: Developmental pathways to recovery among addiction professionals

Overview and rationale

The developmental recovery model presented in this book is based on the idea that recovery is a journey that starts with the escalation of substance use to the point that it has a significant detrimental effect on people's lives to the extent that they aspire to and achieve lasting changes, in their substance use and also in their wider life context.

As discussed in the previous chapters, 'recovery' is a slightly misleading word as it presumes a return to a pre-addiction state, but that is rarely the case as the examples in previous chapters illustrate. In this context, recovery is much more accurately described by the Greek term 'eudaimonia' referring to a 'human flourishing' where the adversity of addiction is not only overcome, it is an essential part of a positive social identity of well-being, carrying with it the sense of living a good life rather than one where hedonistic pleasure is the goal. In this respect, our own findings in a study of people in abstinent recovery from alcohol in Birmingham, England (Hibbert & Best, 2011) that those longer into recovery are 'better than well' (showing higher quality of life than the population norms for social and environmental well-being) are not surprising. In this model, recovery is not merely about overcoming alcohol or drug problems, nor about achieving abstinence, it is about the strengths that are accrued in that journey.

The unfortunate corollary to this is that many, many people who have addiction problems will never achieve recovery for at least two reasons – volition and capacity. Recovery cannot be mandated (unlike treatment) – which may represent a problem for policy-makers, as the model presented here is that recovery is a social identity that involves a self-perception of identity status that, to a greater or lesser extent, is corroborated by peers, family and other key individuals in the life of the individual. The other reason is that many people attempt but never succeed in achieving lasting recovery.

This chapter provides a developmental perspective based on life histories for a group of people who have had some success in undertaking this journey. In the next section, the literature around developmental approaches will be outlined, along with data from studies on addiction careers, before the method and results from the addiction professionals study is presented.

Addiction careers and a developmental perspective

The work of Charles Winick (1961) introduced the idea that drug users 'mature out' of problem substance use, as maturational processes emerge, a claim that would appear to be supported by the work on recovery undertaken in more recent years. Winick reported that the average duration of an addiction career was 8.6 years and that individuals typically 'matured out' of their addiction careers in their mid-30s, either as a result of the length of their addiction career or as part of a lifecycle. Winick's work has been criticised on methodological grounds both in relation to the representativeness of the sample and the criteria used for categorising individuals as having matured out.

In a review for the Centre for Substance Abuse Treatment, Sheedy and Whitter (2009) summed up the existing evidence to estimate that 58% of people who have a lifetime substance dependence will eventually achieve stable recovery, suggesting that recovery is slightly more likely to happen than not. In a more recent analysis, White *et al* (2013) reviewed 415 scientific studies of recovery outcomes (79 community studies, 276 adult clinical studies, and 60 adolescent clinical studies) and found that of adults surveyed in the general population who once met lifetime criteria for substance use disorders, an average of 49.9% (53.9% in studies conducted since 2000) no longer met those criteria at the time of the survey. In community studies reporting both remission rates and abstinence rates for substance use disorders, an average of 43.5% of people who have ever had these disorders achieved remission, but only 17.9% did so through a strategy of complete abstinence (White *et al*, 2013).

However, these overall rates of recovery do not tell us enough about the pathways to recovery in developmental terms. For illicit drugs, much of this work comes from a 33-year outcome study from California. Hser *et al* (2007) found that self-efficacy and psychological well-being were predictors of stable recovery. One of their observations was that career pathways appeared to differ for different substances, with cocaine use increasing through the 20s to early 30s and then declining, but heroin use continuing to increase. In terms of the typology of heroin users developed by Hser *et al* (2007), the authors differentiated between stable high-level users, decelerating users and early quitters. The last group (who constituted just under half of their longitudinal sample) had heroin careers of typically less than 10 years. This early quitting population of heroin users had higher frequencies of use in the first 2–3 years of use but then showed marked reductions and were abstinent by year 11. The authors emphasised key developmental concepts such as trajectories and turning points, although they conceded that there was a dearth of information about cessation factors.

The Californian Civil Addict Programme (CCAP, Hser *et al,* 1993) was a 24-year follow-up study of 581 heroin addicts admitted to a treatment programme between 1962 and 1964 and who were followed up in 1974–1975 and again in 1985–1986. By the second follow-up point, 27.7% had died and a further 25.0% tested negative for opiates (Hser *et al,* 1993). The strongest predictors of mortality in the study were self-reported disability, heavier drinking and smoking, and greater involvement in crime. For many of this cohort, substance use and criminal involvement continued into their 40s, and the authors concluded that if they had not stopped by their late 30s, they were unlikely to do so. Predictors of ongoing substance use at the final follow-up included more polydrug use, heavier criminal involvement and low employment. Among the survivors, rates of treatment engagement were low both among the ongoing substance use and the desistance groups.

More recently, Dennis *et al* (2005) recruited 1,327 participants between 1995 and 1997 from 12 treatment facilities in Chicago and found that the average length of time from substance use initiation to at least one year of abstinence was 27 years (although with a considerable range – of less than 18 to more than 30 years). They found that the time to recovery was longer for those who started earlier, where people take longer to access specialist treatment, where people reported greater psychological distress at the initial treatment, and that most people will need multiple episodes of treatment to achieve stable recovery.

There are a number of treatment outcome studies that have longitudinal data relevant to the current model. From the Drug Abuse Reporting Program

(DARP), a second wave of follow-ups was conducted with a sample of 697 addicts, approximately 12 years after admission, with a follow-up rate of 70% (Simpson & Sells, 1990). Among those patients who had been daily users of opioids before treatment, more than half (53%) reported no daily opioid use at one year. Opioid use continued to decline over time until year six, when it stabilised at 40% for 'any' use and 25% for 'daily' use. At some point during the 12 years following treatment, three-quarters of the sample had relapsed to daily opioid use, but at the year 12 interview, nearly two-thirds (63%) had not used opioids on a daily basis for a period of at least three years.

In the UK, the National Treatment Outcome Research Study (NTORS; Gossop *et al,* 2003) showed significant improvements in recovery outcomes, especially among residential clients. Among the residential patients, almost half (49%) were abstinent from heroin after 4–5 years compared to around one-third of community treatment clients, and the percentage of residential patients who were abstinent from all six illicit target drugs (heroin, crack cocaine, cocaine powder, amphetamine, non-prescribed methadone and non-prescribed benzodiazepines), had increased from one per cent at intake to 38% after 4–5 years. As in the American outcome studies, time in residential treatment was related to improved post-treatment outcomes.

In terms of alcohol outcomes, Vaillant (2003) published a 60-year outcome study of two populations of adolescent males recruited in 1940. The key findings were that by the age of 70 alcohol problems were rare as a result of death or sustained abstinence, and that the best predictors of abstinence were prior alcohol dependence or AA involvement. The study also compared two divergent populations by social status and found that lifetime alcohol abuse was markedly higher (31%) in the urban youth population than in the college population (20%). This sample is linked to the population of delinquents studied by Laub and Sampson (2003) where the core findings were that, as with alcohol problems, delinquency rarely continues to older ages, with the strongest desistance predictors being developing stable and satisfactory relationships and entering employment that the person is happy with.

Thus, there is clear evidence for recovery and for a developmental recovery pathway that is partly predicted on the basis of onset factors and complexity of substance problems, but is more strongly predicted by help-seeking and developmental life events that can be regarded as turning points. This applies particularly to meaningful activities and relationships that bind people to positive personal and social recovery capital.

Timeline follow-backs and the Lifetime Drug Use History (LDUH)

To address the problem of accurately taking a history, Sobell *et al* (1986) developed the Timeline Followback (TLFB) to assist drinkers to record their substance use for periods of up to 18 months, using key 'anchors' like birthdays and major anniversaries to assist with the recording. Their work has shown that the use of the technique has advantages in terms of reliability and coverage, but is time-consuming and can be problematic over longer periods of time (Wennberg & Bohman, 1998).

However, this method is not sufficient and not sufficiently reliable for tracking the stages of a drug-using career and, while working with colleagues in Birmingham and London, we developed and tested the Lifetime Drug Use History (Day *et al,* 2008) to allow tracking of substance use and key life events across the life course, as Skinner and Sheu (1982) had previously done with the Lifetime Drinking History (LDH), which they had shown to be a reliable measure of alcohol consumption across the life course. Similarly, the Life Chart Method (LCM) has been used by psychiatrists to explore the lifetime pattern of relapsing and remitting disorders (Sharpe, 1992).

The Lifetime Drug Use History starts by gathering demographic background information and then collecting summary information on all the substances the person has used problematically in their lifetime, then charts on a grid annual changes in their patterns of use and treatments received. The same timelines are then explored for key life events, such as birth of children, employment history, bereavements and so on. In the initial analysis of the LDUH – undertaken in clinical settings in Birmingham and London – acceptable ratings were achieved for inter-rater and test-retest reliability. The method was also shown to be a more accurate and effective method of mapping key life events than the traditional clinical history taking and was shown to be acceptable to clinicians (Day *et al,* 2008).

In the first research application of the LDUH, Best *et al* (2008) completed 58 LDUH assessments with heroin users to chart their life trajectories and substance use and treatment histories. The average age at the time of interview was around 36 years, and heroin initiation typically occurred at around 21 and daily use at around 23 (for those who transitioned to injecting, this also started at around 23). The time from first use to first treatment seeking was, on average, 7.8 years. Three patterns of heroin use were established using the LDUH method

– an 'intermittent' pattern with gaps and breaks in the use history, an 'escalating' pattern of increasing heroin use, and a 'consistent' pattern of regular consistent quantity and frequency of use. There were gender differences with men typically starting slightly younger but women making a more rapid transition to daily use of heroin. Because this sample was recruited from residential withdrawal treatments, no assumptions can be made about desistance of heroin-using careers.

These two studies demonstrated the acceptability of the method and in the next section we move to assessing the overall addiction and recovery careers of addiction professionals who participated in the study.

The addiction careers of the addiction professionals in the study

At the time of the interviews the mean age of participants was 45.5 years (but this ranged from 34–73 years of age). On average, it was just over 12 years (145 months) since their last use of any substance and slightly longer (an average of 151 months) since their last use of their drug of choice. Nonetheless there was marked variability with time abstinent ranging from around two-and-a-half years up to just over 50 years. All were currently involved in professional activities in the addictions field although their roles and their level of seniority varied markedly.

Not surprisingly, the career patterns differed for primary drinkers to primary illicit drug users – but across the whole population (among those who had engaged in each behaviour), the age of alcohol first use was around 12.5 years, but the age of first daily drinking around the age of 22 years (ranging from 15 to 34). In contrast, for those who used heroin, age of first use was at 22.8 years and first daily use at 23.0 years – in other words, drinking took on average 10 years in this population to reach daily levels while heroin use typically only took a couple of weeks – but that across both groups, daily use was initiated in the early 20s. The overall pattern of drinking careers is shown in **figure 7.1**.

Thus, while the drinking career is longer for the alcohol users, the careers among professionals of alcohol and heroin are remarkably similar with the period of active use through the 20s and stop attempts initiating in the late 20s with desistance typically happening in the early 30s. For the overall sample, the dependent substance-using career starts on average at 21.9 years and ends at 33.3 years – a period of substance dependence of just over 11 years.

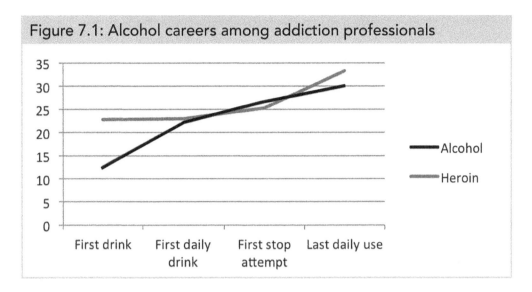

Figure 7.1: Alcohol careers among addiction professionals

This is not markedly different from the heroin users studied in the inpatient unit in the Best *et al* (2008) study of use careers, with the exception of the fact that this group have clearly exited their use careers and have significant periods of stable recovery. This does not mean they are immune to relapse, but that the combination of an average of 12 years since last use and the considerable recovery capital they have built up through social connectedness, employment and significant life changes, would suggest a stable transition.

How this group does differ is that they have extensive work experience – averaging 14.8 years of full-time employment, with some of this occurring before and during the period of active addiction for some of the group, although this is rarely unbroken. They are also generally educated – averaging 4.3 years of college or university – although it is important to say that for just under half of the sample that tertiary education has taken place since the start of their recovery journey. Although the sample report relatively late onset of dependence – they left school early on average (16.6 years) and with an average of only 4.5 years of secondary education, indicating low rates of immediate transition to college and university. There is also some domestic stability – around two-thirds report ever being married or co-habiting for an average of 15.6 years – although this was frequently disrupted during the years of active addiction, and for most of the participants current relationships post-date the start of their recovery journey, with just under half of the sample having been through divorce and three participants having been divorced twice or more.

In terms of life adversities, this is a group that has experienced multiple adversities. Forty per cent of the group had at least one episode of homelessness during their addiction careers, and those that had been homeless had experienced just over one year of homelessness on average. They had been hospitalised on average on 1.6 occasions and had experienced an average of 1.1 bereavements. With regard to criminal justice, 31.8% of the addiction professionals had ever been in prison, averaging 5.1 years of prison time, with age of first imprisonment averaging at 25.3 years and age of most recent prison time at 31.3 years. Over half of the sample (54.5%) had ever been arrested and just under half had ever been convicted. The mean age of first arrest was 21.8 years but the age of first conviction was 18.3 years (this shows that those who got arrested without charge were typically significantly older at that point).

The treatment and recovery careers of the addiction professionals

There were inconsistencies in formal treatment experience in the addiction professionals' recovery career – with just over half having accessed formal treatment, with the most common form of treatment received being residential rehabilitation (62.5%), followed by residential detoxification (41.7%). **Figure 7.2** provides an overview of the history of initial and most recent engagement with community and residential treatment and mutual aid groups.

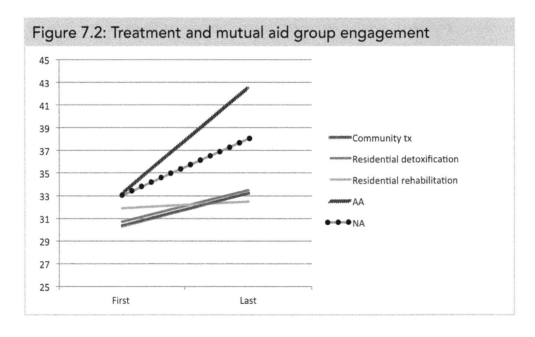

Figure 7.2: Treatment and mutual aid group engagement

As can be seen in **figure 7.2**, there is a fairly narrow window for formal treatment with all three modalities of treatment typically occurring within a fairly narrow time period – in other words, for this group of successful recovery graduates, where community treatment has been needed, it is required for a mean of only three years, which is markedly lower than that reported in the ongoing treatment careers reported by Best *et al* (2008).

It is also apparent from the graph that there is a progression from treatment to mutual aid group involvement with the completion of formal treatment – where it is required – paving the way for mutual aid group participation, something that is much more common in the sample. In total, 91.7% of participants reported active involvement with the 12-step groups, either AA or NA or both with the average time spent in AA 8.6 years (and a range of 1–21 years) and the average time spent in NA of 5.1 years (and a range of 1–13 years). Although not all of those involved in 12-step groups had continued their involvement at the time of the interview, single episodes of engagement were most common – very few participants re-commenced 12-step group involvement after stopping attending.

The self-reported age for beginning the recovery journey is 33.8 years coinciding with the completion of formal treatment and the initiation of 12-step involvement for the majority of addiction professionals participating in the study. It is also important to note that engagement with 12-step was frequently initiated through treatment – detoxification but particularly residential rehabilitation – so there is a strong sense that formal treatment can open a window of opportunity for change but that the ongoing support needed to sustain that change will come from engagement in mutual aid groups. The relationship this has to identity is discussed in more detail in the discussion at the end of this chapter and then again in Chapter 9.

Turning points and trajectories

There is a clear behavioural pathway to recovery for the majority of the addiction professionals, which involves residential rehabilitation treatment followed by engagement in the mutual aid fellowships – with this primarily involving AA, NA or both, either on an ongoing basis or for a fixed period of time. However, underpinning this process is an event-driven model that is generally consistent with the findings from Best *et al* (2008) where there is a cumulative 'maturing out' characterised as having had enough coupled with one or more trigger events that elicited help-seeking as indicated in the stories in Chapter 6.

While the life events that triggered problematic substance use were primarily adverse life events – serious illness (n=8), the death or illness of a partner (n=6), separation from a partner (n=4), death or illness of a parent or other relative (n=8), the reported trigger events for initiating the recovery journey are markedly different. The mean age that the recovery journey began was at an average of 33.8 years and participants described up to three key turning points that occurred around the time of the recovery journey – these included the threat of negative events (about to lose a job or to lose a partner, fears about mental health including suicide, and getting into trouble with the law), but it also included opportunities. These included getting a job, the start of a new relationship, seeing other people move into recovery and being inspired by that, and the birth of children.

Thus, among the professionals, both positive and negative events generally combined with a gradual 'falling out of love' with the substance and the related lifestyle (consistent with a maturing out model) and the opening of a window of opportunity. That window of opportunity typically involved access to rehabilitation, personal therapy or 12-step groups, but was also about the development of a new identity as partner, parent, worker or volunteer. The developmental model here for the professionals is of a gradual dissatisfaction with an addiction lifestyle – typically around 10 years or so after commencing – brought to a head by a turning point that created a window of opportunity for change that the person was able to take advantage of, resulting in a 'recovery spin' through which personal and social recovery capital was nurtured and sustained through social support for recovery and which enabled a new social identity to emerge, in many cases a complex and multifaceted identity with recovery as a core but not exclusive aspect.

For our addiction professionals, the average length of time from the onset of dependence to the start of the recovery journey averaged 11.1 years (but with a range of 2–21 years). Female addiction careers were slightly longer than male careers (12.1 years compared to 10.5 years) but this difference was not significant. Similarly, those who had ever been to prison had slightly longer addiction careers than those who had not (12.1 years compared to 10.6 years) but again this was not significant. However, those who regarded themselves as currently 'in recovery' typically had longer addiction careers (an average of 12.1 years) than those who regarded their addiction careers as complete (average of 8.3 years) and this difference was statistically significant. Further analysis will be presented in Chapter 8 about the relationships between career factors and the well-being of the individual at the time of the interview.

Interpreting the addiction and recovery careers of the addiction professionals

The onset of addiction problems typically started in this group in their early 20s and resulted in an active addiction career to the early 30s with the self-identified start of the recovery journey typically being around the age of 33, although with considerable variability across the group and also marked differences in the duration of their recovery journeys to date.

As early as Winick's (1961) work, there has been debate about whether 'maturing out' happens and, if so, whether this is a consequence of ageing or whether it is precipitated by other lifestyle factors and key events. As with previous studies of recovery (Biernacki, 1986; McIntosh & McKeganey, 2002; Best *et al*, 2008), there are some indications that this happens, but the variability of the timing of recovery within each sample would suggest that while it may be a necessary condition it is not sufficient, and that internal changes may still require trigger events to precipitate recovery.

Across a range of substances and backgrounds, the current group of high-functioning addiction professionals reported a wide range of key life events that were triggers for the start of their recovery journeys. However, these were not necessarily the first 'major' life events these individuals had experienced – many already had children, had previous and ongoing relationships and jobs, and had experienced bereavements and significant physical and psychological illness. However, it is the coming together of three elements that would appear to create a positive recovery trajectory:

1. a readiness to make the transition to recovery
2. a trigger event that generates the window of opportunity for change
3. the availability of therapeutic or peer supports that can nurture existing recovery capital and generate new recovery resources.

The third of the points above is really the bridge to sustaining that initial effort – and the issue of emerging recovery capital, social identity change and 'recovery spin' is addressed in more detail in Chapter 8. From a developmental perspective, the remainder of this chapter will be devoted to addressing the three key aspects of prolonging and sustaining recovery careers – treatment and overcoming acute addiction, sustaining those gains on the return to the community and transitioning to 'stable recovery'.

Although a number of participants had some experience of community treatment – including a small number who had received substitute prescribing at some point in their recovery journeys – it would appear that the intervention that was sufficiently intensive to create a 'turning point' in their addiction careers was residential treatment, and particularly residential rehabilitation treatment. Perhaps, surprisingly, several of the participants spoke of residential rehabilitation as not only beneficial but also as an enjoyable and positive life experience. The time spent in rehabilitation and the focus, especially in therapeutic communities, on fundamentally addressing identity through teaching 'right living' (De Leon, 2000) is entirely compatible with a significant turning point. It is also noticeable that most of those who attended rehabilitation had only one episode, and so, in this population, clearly associated with the conditions for a 'turning point' in not only the addiction career but also the wider life trajectory.

However, as has been clearly evidenced in studies of the effectiveness of residential rehabilitation, it is the continuity of care that is associated with the long-term benefits and changes (Messina *et al,* 2006). Not only is this consistent with a model of care continuity, it is also consistent with a recovery model in which specialist services are not sufficient and need to be linked to community-based and peer-driven recovery interventions. The current study provides support for one particular form of continuous care, the mutual aid groups of Alcoholics Anonymous and Narcotics Anonymous. While there is clear evidence that mutual aid attendance significantly enhances treatment outcomes (Zemore & Subbaraman, 2013), this study suggests that residential treatment acts as a trigger to mutual aid engagement. As residential services will often struggle to provide adequate aftercare, particularly if clients are recruited from and return to geographically dispersed towns and cities, active engagement in community recovery supports and resources will be essential to support the ongoing recovery journey. Even for those with prior experience of AA or NA, the re-initiation of contact during or immediately following residential treatment would appear to have made those individuals more receptive to active engagement in the 12-step groups.

However, the recovering professionals did diverge in the length of time this mutual aid group involvement continued, with a roughly equal split between those whose engagement continued to the time of the interview and those whose involvement was time limited. This difference is also associated with the split between those who see themselves as still in recovery and those who see themselves as recovered. For some individuals, and this is more typically the case for males and for alcoholics than heroin addicts, active engagement in the programme is an essential requirement in their ongoing recovery journey.

Female professionals and ex-heroin addicts are much more likely to see 12-step involvement as a crucial stepping stone in their recovery pathway but one that they become less reliant on as their recovery journey progresses. The implications for both recovery capital and for social identity in recovery are addressed in Chapter 9.

Conclusion

The histories given by the addiction professionals provide further evidence that while recovery is a personal story of individual change and growth, there are also some common biographical and developmental components to that journey. For this population, the onset of dependence typically occurred in the early 20s and recovery typically started in the early 30s. Pathways to recovery were also variable but typically the addiction professionals interviewed for this book had a number of failed attempts at stopping (either by themselves or through short-term residential or community treatments) before successfully ending their active addiction careers. There was typically a gradual change in relationship to the substance-using lifestyle and a trigger event that precipitated some form of active help-seeking that generated a sustainable turning point. That turning point involved significant life changes (relocation and often extensive time in residential treatment) linking to ongoing support through mutual aid before recovery stabilised. Long-term recovery was sustained either through continuing engagement in mutual aid or transitioning to an identity as an 'ex-addict'.

References

Best D, Day E, Cantillano V, Lopez Gaston R, Nambamali A & Keaney F (2008) Mapping heroin careers: utilising a standardised history-taking method to assess the speed of escalation of heroin using careers in a treatment-seeking cohort. *Drug and Alcohol Review* **27** 165–170.

Biernacki P (1986) *Pathways from Heroin Addiction: Recovery without treatment*. Philadelphia, PA: Temple University Press.

Day E, Best D, Cantillano V, Lopez Gaston R, Nambamali A & Keaney F (2008) Measuring the use and career histories of drug users in treatment: Reliability of the Lifetime Drug Use History (LDUH) and its data yield relative to clinical case notes. *Drug and Alcohol Review* **27** 171–177.

De Leon G (2000) *The Therapeutic Community: Theory, model and method*. New York: Springer.

Dennis M, Scott C, Funk R & Foss M (2005) The duration and correlates of addiction and treatment careers. *Journal of Substance Abuse Treatment* **28** 851–862.

Gossop M, Marsden J, Stewart D & Kidd T (2003) The National Treatment Outcome Research Study (NTORS): 4-5 year follow-up results. *Addiction* **98** 291–303.

Hibbert L & Best D (2011) Assessing recovery and functioning in former problem drinkers at different stages of their recovery journey. *Drug and Alcohol Review* **30** 12–20.

Hser Y-I, Anglin D & Powers K (1993) A 24-year follow-up of California narcotics addicts. *Archives of General Psychiatry* **50** (7) 577–584.

Hser Y, Longshore D & Anglin M (2007) The life course perspective on drug use: a conceptual framework for understanding drug use. *Trajectories Evaluation Review* **31** 515–547.

Laub J & Sampson R (2003) *Shared Beginnings, Divergent Lives: Delinquent boys to age 70*. Cambridge, Mass: Harvard University Press.

McIntosh J & McKeganey N (2002) *Beating the Dragon: The recovery from dependent drug use*. Harlow, Essex: Pearson Education.

Messina N, Burdon W, Hagopian G & Prendergast M (2006) Predictors of prison-based treatment outcomes: a comparison of men and women participants. *American Journal of Drug and Alcohol Abuse* **32** 7–28.

Sharpe M (1992) The life chart: Historical curiosity or modern clinical tool. In: K Hawton & P Cowen (eds) *Practical Problems in Clinical Psychiatry*, p222–230. Oxford: Oxford University Press.

Sheedy C K & Whitter M (2009) *Guiding Principles and Elements of Recovery-Oriented Systems of Care: What Do We Know From the Research?* HHS Publication No. (SMA) 09-4439. Rockville, MD: Center for Substance Abuse Treatment, Substance Abuse and Mental Health Services Administration.

Skinner H & Sheu W (1982) Reliability of alcohol use indices: the Lifetime Drinking History and the MAST. *Journal of Studies on Alcohol* **43** 1157–1170.

Simpson D & Sells S (1990) *Opioid Addiction and Treatment*. Malabar: Krieger.

Sobell M, Sobell L, Klajner F, Pavan D & Basian E (1986) The reliability of a timeline method for assessing normal drinker college students' recent drinking history: utility for alcohol research. *Addictive Behaviours* **11** 149–161.

Vaillant G (2003) A 60-year follow-up of alcoholic men. *Addiction* **98** 1043–1051.

Wennberg P & Bohman M (1998) The timeline follow back technique: psychometric properties of a 28-day timeline for measuring alcohol consumption. *German Journal of Psychiatry* **2** 62–68.

White W, Weingartner R, Levine M, Evans A & Lamb R (2013) Recovery prevalence and health profile of people in recovery: results of a Southeastern Pennsylvania survey on the resolution of alcohol and other drug problems. *Journal of Psychoactive Drugs* **45** (4) 287–296.

Winick C (1961) Maturing out of narcotic addiction. *Bulletin on Narcotics* **14** (1) 1–7.

Zemore S & Subbaraman M (2013) Involvement in 12-step activities and treatment outcomes. *Substance Abuse* **34** 60–69.

Chapter 8: The recovery capital of addiction professionals and its relationship to well-being

This chapter completes the analysis of the recovery stories from addiction professionals and examines the issue of current functioning and well-being. This is a group of people who have all described themselves as being in recovery and the chapter will examine what that means in terms of ongoing pathology and illness factors, but it will also address the question of the strengths and assets the person has, in terms of both quality of life and recovery assets. The first section of the chapter will briefly review the debate around what recovery means in terms of well-being and functioning, before examining the literature around an assets or capital-based approach to recovery. Then data will be summarised in each of these domains from the addiction professionals and this will be discussed in terms of the existing literature and evidence.

Definitions of recovery

Two national consensus groups (Betty Ford Consensus Group, 2007; UK Drug Policy Commission, 2007) and one international expert (White, 2009) have all offered definitions of what we mean by recovery with each of three definitions involving three common elements – health, sobriety, and citizenship. The Betty Ford Institute Consensus Group go on to describe three stages to recovery journeys – an 'early' stage of up to three years, 'sustained' recovery of between 3–5 years and 'stable' recovery of more than five years, reflecting the prolonged time-course believed to be required for recovery to stabilise (White & Kurtz, 2006).

As discussed in Best (2012), the problem with this definition is that it creates the risk that the 'ownership' of recovery does not rest with the individual but with some externally imposed threshold – that recovery is not experiential, rather it is the absence of problems – no health symptoms, no substance use and no benefit claims. For this reason, it is important to ensure that there is an experiential and positive component to the recovery experience – as promoted by Deegan (1998) who argued that: '*Recovery refers to the lived experience of people as they accept and overcome the challenge of disability … they experience themselves as recovering a new sense of self and of purpose within and beyond the limits of the disability*'.

For the purposes of the current sample of addiction professionals this provokes three questions – the first about the impact of the duration of recovery, the second about subjective and objective markers of recovery, and the third about recovery assets or strengths. Although the majority of the sample is in long-term recovery, there are a number of people in the study with less than five years of recovery time and the chapter will assess the impact of recovery duration on pathologies and strengths. The second question will look at the issue of ongoing substance use, physical and psychological health symptoms, and quality of life. The community engagement aspect of the consensus definitions will be assessed in terms of education and employment questions. The specific issues and questions around strengths and recovery capital are outlined in the next section.

Recovery capital

The background to recovery capital has been outlined in Chapters 2 and 3 and will not be repeated here in detail. The key point is that the current study provides an opportunity to look at the extent of overlap between recovery capital measured on the Assessment of Recovery Capital (ARC; Groshkova *et al*, 2012) and the WHO Brief Quality of Life measure (Skevington *et al*, 2004). We will also be able to assess the overlap between the ARC measure of social and personal recovery capital and ongoing symptoms for physical and psychological health measured by the Maudsley Addiction Profile sub-scales (Marsden *et al*, 1998). The aim here is to see if there are clear inverse associations between pathologies and strengths, or as would be implied by the Deegan definitions of mental health recovery, that quality of life and recovery can continue to grow irrespective of continuing symptoms.

Furthermore, the chapter will report the association between participation in recovery communities and recovery capital and quality of life. The Recovery Group Participation Scale (Groshkova *et al*, 2011) will be used as a measure of both immersion in recovery communities and as a proxy indicator of community recovery capital, along with the number of people in recovery in the individual's social network. The key questions in this section will be about the relationship between quality of life and different aspects of recovery capital and its links to recovery community engagement.

Recovery duration

On average, the professionals had been in recovery for just over 11 years with a range of three to 32 years suggesting considerable variability in their recovery experiences, and this was reflected in their behaviours.

The first major difference was recovery group participation – those who had less than five years in recovery had almost twice as high a score on the Recovery Group Participation Scale (mean of around 12 out of 14) as those who had more than five years in recovery (mean of 6.6 out of 14), and this difference was statistically significant. This may suggest that early in recovery it is more important to be actively involved in recovery groups and activities, and that, for this group of people, that becomes less salient as their recovery becomes more established and other identities and roles emerge. This fits with a model where individuals identify strongly with recovery groups and communities early in their recovery journeys but, as their personal capital grows, and their networks expand to a diverse range of non-using groups, so their reliance on recovery groups for social support – and for a positive social identity – may diminish.

Although there were no overall significant differences in recovery capital on the ARC (nor in the domains of Personal and Social) people with more than five years in recovery reported slightly stronger coping skills and higher ratings of safety and satisfaction in their homes. There were no clear differences in the WHOQOL brief scale comparing those with more or less than five years in recovery.

Entirely consistent with the theory of recovery duration and ongoing well-being – as articulated previously in our study of drinkers in long-term recovery in Birmingham (Hibbert & Best, 2011), those who were less than five years into their recovery journey had higher levels of anxiety, depression and physical health problems (with the last effect reaching statistical significance). As previously reported, long-term recovery is associated with marked improvements in physical and psychological well-being.

Also consistent with the Hibbert and Best paper is the finding that in terms of well-being the five-year cut-off is an artificial one and when assessed as a continuous variable there are clear relationships between recovery time and personal recovery capital, and three of the four quality of life domains – physical, psychological and social. There was only a weak association to social recovery capital, but the overall implication is clear that recovery continues to grow over time. While White and Kurtz (2006) have argued that five years is around the time that relapse risk reaches its lowest level probabilistically, this is not the same as saying that this is the end of the growth of recovery benefit and what the current findings would suggest is that individuals continue to accrue recovery capital even if they do not persist with active engagement in recovery groups and communities – or at least do so to a much lesser extent.

Personal experiences of well-being

Hawthorne *et al* (2006) have published population norms for the World Health Organization Brief Quality of Life measure and these are shown in **table 8.1** compared to the mean scores reported by the addiction professionals in recovery.

Table 8.1: WHOQOL-BREF scores for population norms and addiction professionals in recovery			
Domain	Addiction professionals	Population norm scores	Hibbert and Best (2011) stable recovery group
Physical	86.7 (± 10.7)	73.5 (±18.1)	78.5 (±22.4)
Psychological	73.9 (± 9.8)	70.6 (± 14.0)	77.3 (±15.5)
Social	76.2 (± 13.5)	71.5 (± 18.2)	87.9 (±15.0)
Environmental	85.2 (± 10.1)	75.1 (± 13.0)	86.1 (±10.0)

In other words, the addiction professionals exceed the population norm scores for well-being in all four of the dimensions of the WHOQOL-BREF markedly so for physical and environmental quality of life – they are high on all of the dimensions but noticeably reporting positive physical well-being and satisfaction with their place in their neighbourhoods. This is particularly important given that many reported a range of other health problems and some residual health consequences of their substance-using careers.

However, the results from the addiction professionals are slightly different from those reported in Hibbert and Best (2011) for the stable recovery group who were more than five years since their last drink. The domain scores are comparable for psychological and environmental quality of life, are higher in physical quality of life but lower in social quality of life. This may reflect the inclusion of the earlier stage recovery professionals or the impact of including former heroin users as well as the alcoholics that were the sole focus of the Birmingham study. Nonetheless, the mean score remains higher than for the general public, and this provides some further, albeit, more cautious, support for the idea of stable recovery as reflecting a 'better than well' state.

In spite of the high levels of quality of life there was still some evidence in the sample of residual psychological and physical health problems – with a mean score of 2.5 (±2.2) for anxiety (in a scale out of 20) and of 1.3 (±1.7) for depression. For physical health symptoms, the mean score was 5.3 (±3.1) out of 40. These are low scores and are not indicative of significant ongoing pathologies. Not surprisingly, health symptoms was inversely related to physical quality of life (and this was strongly significant in statistical terms), but higher levels of depression were associated with lower social quality of life. Satisfaction with the person's lived environment was also inversely associated with both anxiety and with physical health symptoms.

Thus, there is some relationship between aspects of quality of life and physical and psychological symptoms but the relationships are not strong and this issue will be explored in more depth in the next section on recovery capital.

Recovery capital and assets

The basic pattern of recovery strengths in each of the 10 sub-scales along with the standard deviations is shown in **table 8.2**.

Table 8.2: ARC sub-scale scores in addiction professionals

Sub-scale	Mean	SD
Sobriety and substance use	4.7	0.5
Psychological health	4.7	0.4
Physical health	4.5	0.7
Meaningful activity	4.5	0.8
Recovery experiences	5.0	0
Risk	4.2	0.8
Coping	4.5	0.9
Social support	4.3	0.9
Housing and safety	4.7	0.5
Citizenship	4.4	0.8

The addiction professionals in recovery reported consistently high scores across all of the dimensions ranging from a maximum possible average of 5.0 for recovery experiences to 4.2 for risk. There is a risk in this group that the ARC is not the right instrument as there is a 'ceiling effect' where people successfully in work and safely in their recovery reported scores around the maximum possible for each scale. The overall total score averages 45.4 out of 50, consisting of averages of 22.9 (out of 25) for personal recovery capital and 22.6 (out of 25) for social recovery capital.

There are negative associations between the overall recovery capital score on the ARC and the measures of physical and psychological health, with this particularly strong, and statistically significant, for anxiety, and this relates particularly to personal recovery capital (measuring as it does, psychological recovery capital as one of the sub-scales). This is consistent with the theory that recovery capital is associated with lower level of symptoms but that it is not a mirror image – in other words, people do report very high levels of recovery capital while still having some kind of continuing health symptoms. However, it is important to note that none of the existing sample were actively using any form of illicit drug or alcohol so the relationship between 'controlled' use and recovery capital could not have been tested in this population. However, it is telling that the addiction professionals in long-term recovery, all of whom were functioning highly and reporting positive life quality, were completely abstinent and there was no evidence of controlled use.

There is a much stronger positive association between recovery capital and quality of life with the personal capital measure strongly linked to all four of the WHOQOL domains. The relationship for social capital was weaker with this significantly associated with only social and environmental quality of life. There is no relationship between recovery capital and the duration of the recovery career suggesting that recovery is more about the here and now, and the individual's life circumstances, and that for those who do manage to achieve recovery it is the current circumstances and duration of recovery that are important not the historical factors of the duration or severity of the addiction career. However, the high scores and the possibility of a ceiling effect means that there is not the variability in scores to adequately test associations.

In terms of specific scales there were very strong inverse relationships between reported citizenship and both the number of people in recovery in the social network and the number of users in the social network. Given the above findings, what this might suggest is that for those who become more actively involved in non-recovery specific activities there is a reduction in their involvement with groups and individuals linked to addiction but also linked to formal recovery. This is consistent with the idea advanced by William White (2007) that for some people mutual aid involvement is a stepping stone to non-recovery related social networks and activities.

The citizenship sub-scale is also strongly linked with environmental quality of life and inversely with both anxiety and health symptoms, suggesting that this is a particularly important measure for stable and ongoing recovery. There was also a strong and consistent relationship between scores on the coping sub-scale of the ARC and three of the four quality of life measures – physical, psychological and social quality of life. This would suggest the emergence of recovery coping skills as suggested by Moos (2007) is linked to the growth of well-being in a range of domains. However, as these findings are correlational, it is important to note that all inferences of cause are inevitably speculative.

What is the significance of ongoing involvement in recovery activities?

The addiction recovery professionals' questionnaire had two items that dealt specifically with this issue – Recovery Group Participation Scale score and current social group membership.

To start with the RGPS scale as a total, the mean score was 7.3 (with a range of 0–13) on a scale out of 14, suggesting reasonable variability in this sample. RGPS score was only weakly associated with scores on personal and social recovery possibly reflecting the generally high scores in this domain, and the fact that recovery group involvement was typically much higher among those earlier in their recovery journeys (as reported above). It was associated with having more people in recovery in the social network, but had no impact on the other two social measures – number of people who were either users or non-users in the social network. This is consistent with the fact that it was more common among professionals in recovery who were younger and also those who reported slightly higher levels of anxiety and depression. It did not relate to quality of life measures and overall was not a strong predictor of any of the other well-being factors.

The second measure that is relevant here is the report of current involvement with different populations as reported in **table 8.3**.

Table 8.3: Current social network by using status		
Group	Mean	Range
Non-users	12.0	2–30
People in recovery	14.7	2–100
Active users	2.0	0–40

The social networks of professionals in recovery consists largely of people who have never had addiction problems and people who are currently in recovery, with only a quarter of the professionals having social contact with active users outside of the working environment. This meant that the average total network size reported by the participants was 28.6, suggesting a high degree of social embeddedness.

It is interesting to note that the people with the larger social networks had higher levels of anxiety and lower levels of physical and environmental quality of life, and that these effects were not influenced by the length of time in recovery. So, contrary to the effects that would be expected about the social benefits of networks, there is an adverse effect among professionals that will be discussed in the section below.

Overview of well-being in recovery professionals

For the addiction professionals interviewed in the current study, the most obvious common characteristics are complete sobriety – not one of the participants are engaged in recreational or controlled substance use – and social connectedness. In spite of their roles as addiction professionals, not all were open about their recovery status and not all had extensive recovery-focused social networks. Only a quarter of the group had any form of social contact with people who were current substance users, suggesting detachment from the substance-using world – including that of drinkers – and for some, this also involved moving away from overt recovery groups and communities. Recovery did not mean 'remission' for all of the participants in that many reported symptoms of psychological distress or physical health ailments, although it is important to say that for many the maladies experienced, particularly the physical illnesses, were nothing to do with their substance use. However, the participants would generally fulfil the thresholds set by the Betty Ford Consensus Group (2007) and the UK Drug Policy Commission (2007) of sobriety, citizenship and global health. Crucially, they all additionally spoke of a personal and subjective transformation of identity and well-being that was personal and consistent with Deegan's 'lived experience' model (Deegan, 1998).

Overall, the addiction professionals reported very high levels of recovery capital – in the original ARC paper with a clinical sample, the mean overall ARC score was 31.3 (Groshkova *et al,* 2012) in a clinical population and, in a visible recovery community in three English towns, the mean recovery capital score was 42.1 (Best *et al,* 2013), with the current sample of addiction professionals in recovery reporting a mean score of 45.4. In the Best *et al* paper (2013), there were three factors that predicted recovery capital in the visible recovery communities – time in recovery, social networks and involvement in recovery groups. Only the first of these showed any similar effect in the addiction professionals with more ambivalent attitudes reported both to visibility and to immersion in recovery activities. Growing recovery capital is still associated with longer time in recovery, and what the current study suggests is a developmental model that diverges in this population partly based on whether the individuals continue to engage in mutual aid group activities and the linked question of their self-identity as still in recovery or as recovered.

A more complex question is about the relationship between recovery and recovery capital on the one hand and 'remission' on the other. Warner (2010) has argued that only around 20% of those with severe and enduring mental illness will achieve full 'remission'. Among the addiction professionals there is remission from substance use, but not always from the associated mental health and life problems, whether they are aetiologically linked to the substance use or not. For some individuals, particularly those in earlier recovery, the resolution of the substance use component of their addiction has been adequately resolved but challenges remain around psychological and physical health and around lifestyles and relationships. It is clear that there is a strong association between recovery capital and quality of life and an inverse relationship between recovery capital and physical and psychiatric symptoms. This may suggest that the development of recovery capital provides the resources and supports to overcome these obstacles and challenges – and collectively will provide the resilience skills needed for the continuing growth and life journey.

Probably the most fascinating and unexpected result of the current findings – and one that will require further research to unpick – is the relationship between recovery progress and involvement with mutual aid and other recovery groups. Overall, there were mixed levels of recovery group participation at the time of the interviews, although almost all of the professionals in recovery had had extensive mutual aid group involvement early in their recovery careers. With this group in particular, the emergence of a recovery identity as 'in recovery' or 'recovered' may not only be about their biography – and the general tenor of the developmental model presented here would suggest not – but more about their current situation and working roles. Particularly for those currently employed in residential and TC treatment models, the emergence of a recovered identity may supersede the 'in recovery' identity and ease the transition to a new set of social rules, norms and so a resulting social identity of recovery (Jetten *et al*, 2009).

In this population, the social networks are large and diverse – with around half of the people in the social network being in recovery. Those who were currently in mutual aid groups both had a larger social network overall, had a larger proportion of people in recovery in their social networks and had greater participation in current recovery activities, and this represented just over half of the addiction professionals surveyed. Mutual aid participation is clearly not a necessity for continuing recovery in this group at least but it has a huge role to play in the recovery journeys of professionals if not in their current identities. Those who move away from the mutual aid fellowships will typically have smaller social networks but these are more likely to be diverse and so potentially offer a more socially protective benefit by providing multiple identities that the individual can draw on – and this may be particularly important where recovery is stigmatised (Phillips & Shaw, 2013) and so the individual needs to be able to present alternative social identities contingent on the context.

In the Hibbert and Best study (2011) we raised the possibility that participants were 'better than well' as a result of their transition to stable recovery. A similar conclusion can be derived from the existing group as well not only as a consequence of the quality of life scores that exceed population norms but also because of the exceptionally high recovery capital scores and social connectedness reported by this population. This provides further empirical support for the suggestion that recovery has little to do with a return to a pre-addiction state but that recovery is a personal journey of growth that, as a consequence of the struggles it entails and the resilience and self-discovery it necessitates, will afford the opportunity of a satisfaction and quality of life that is beyond what many people who have not come through such a journey could experience.

Conclusion

The addiction professionals have provided further evidence that recovery capital continues to grow over the recovery journey and for this group, embedded in citizenship and consistent in their sobriety, there is exceptionally high recovery capital that is linked to a positive quality of life and few residual symptoms and problems. Their recovery journeys, and so their profiles of strength and resilience, are not all the same and this is reflected in diverging beliefs about continuing recovery group participation and about social identity, which will be explored further in Chapter 9.

References

Best D (2012) *Addiction Recovery: A movement for personal change and social growth in the UK.* Brighton: Pavilion.

Best D, Honor S, Karpusheff J, Loudon L, Hall R, Groshkova T & White W (2013) Wellbeing and recovery functioning among substance users engaged in post-treatment recovery support groups. *Alcoholism Treatment Quarterly* **30** (4) 397–406.

Betty Ford Institute Consensus Group (2007) What is recovery? A working definition from the Betty Ford Institute. *Journal of Substance Abuse Treatment* **33** 221–228.

Deegan P (1998) Recovery: the lived experience of rehabilitation. *Psychosocial Rehabilitation Journal* **11** 11–19.

Groshkova T, Best D & White W (2011) Recovery Group Participation Scale (RGPS): factor structure in alcohol and heroin recovery populations. *Journal of Groups in Addiction and Recovery* **6** 76–92.

Groshkova T, Best D & White W (2012) The Assessment of Recovery Capital: Properties and psychometrics of a measure of addiction recovery strengths. *Drug and Alcohol Review* **32** (2) 187–194.

Hawthorne G, Herrman H & Murphy B (2006) Interpreting the WHOQOL-BREF; Preliminary population norms and effect sizes. *Social Indicators Research* **77** 37–59.

Hibbert L & Best D (2011) Assessing recovery and functioning in former problem drinkers at different stages of their recovery journey. *Drug and Alcohol Review* **30** 12–20.

Jetten J, Haslam SA, Iyer A & Haslam C (2009) Turning to others in times of change: Shared identity and coping with stress. In: S Stürmer and M Snyder (Eds) *New Directions in the Study of Helping: Group-level perspectives on motivations, consequences and interventions* (pp 139–156). Chichester: Wiley-Blackwell.

Marsden J, Stewart D, Farrell M, Best D & Gossop M (1998) *The Maudsley Addiction Profile*. London: NAC/IP.

Moos R (2007) Theory-based active ingredients of effective treatments for substance use disorders. *Drug and Alcohol Dependence* **88** (2–3) 109–121.

Phillips L & Shaw A (2013) Substance use more stigmatised than smoking and obesity. *Journal of Substance Use* **18** (4) 247–253.

Skevington S, Lotfy M & O'Connell K (2004) The World Health Organisation's WHOQOL-BREF quality of life assessment: Psychometric properties and results of the international field trial. A report from the WHOQOL group. *Quality of Life Research* **13** 299–310.

UK Drug Policy Commission Consensus Group (2007) *Developing a Vision of Recovery: A work in progress*. UKDPC: London.

Warner R (2010) Does the scientific model support the recovery model? *The Psychiatrist* **34** 3–5.

White W (2007) *Peer-based Recovery Support Systems*. Pittsburgh, PA: Northeast Addiction Technology Transfer Center, Great Lakes Addiction Technology Transfer Center, Philadelphia Department of Behavioral Health & Mental Retardation Services.

White WL (2009) The mobilization of community resources to support long-term addiction recovery. *Journal of Substance Abuse Treatment* **36** (2) 146–158. doi: 10.1016/j.jsat.2008.10.006.

White W & Kurtz E (2006) The varieties of recovery experience. *International Journal of Self Help and Self Care* **3** (1–2) 21–61.

Chapter 9: Recovery and the developmental model of change

This chapter will review the developmental model of recovery and the explicit focus on social identity change in the light of the findings presented in Chapters 3–8 based on the studies in Glasgow, Victoria and the final Australian and UK study of addiction professionals in recovery. The key point of this chapter is to review and amend the model outlined of how people initiate but particularly about continuing and sustaining the initial recovery efforts.

Assumptions and beginnings

Although this is not a story about natural recovery, there is no assumption made that formal treatment is a necessary foundation for recovery. It is assumed that there is a developmental change that occurs that enables individuals to start a recovery journey. There will be very little discussion of the techniques of treatment for two reasons – they are already the subject of a large literature around 'what works' in talking therapies, in pharmacotherapies and around community and residential settings – but also because the emphasis of this book is that developmental turning points are about fundamental life changes for the individual, both in the subjective and phenomenal world and in terms of the lived environment of families, friendship networks and communities. In other words, the emphasis here is on subjective experience, and positive strengths, and so there will be little focus on reduction in symptoms and adverse health experiences.

In our 2008 paper, based on a group consisting of many addiction professionals (Best *et al*, 2008), we argued that the initiation of a recovery journey was often triggered by a combination of changing attitudes towards substance use ('tired of the lifestyle') that created a general openness to change but that the trigger was an individual event or a series of events. This is consistent with the 'maturing out' idea advanced by Winick as early as 1961, but also by the ideas of Neal Shover (1985) in his work on ageing criminals. This is based on the idea that, as individuals age, so their capacity for risk taking and their fear of the consequences of risky behaviours shifts in a more conservative direction that is also linked to growing responsibilities around families and partners. There is some evidence of this in the sample with a 'typical' biographical pattern of adolescent experimentation followed by the development of problem use in the early 20s and the beginning of the recovery journey in the early 30s. However, this masks significant individual variation in the life course and the central argument advanced here is that this individual variability is event-focused and not based on some kind of biological or biographical maturation.

This is consistent with the developmental notion of turning points and trajectories developed by Hser *et al* (2007). Their point is that there are life trajectories (such as falling into and out of love with substances and the related lifestyle) but that there are key life events that create turning points that can fundamentally alter persisting trajectories. To return to theories of crime and delinquency, the Rochester Youth Development Study (Thornberry *et al,* 2003) is based on a general community sample that reported multiple delinquency careers including a 'late bloomer group' who do not fit so well with theories of risk factors and adolescent onset. Thornberry's interaction model would suggest that early risk factors (such as poor parental monitoring, early school exclusion and antisocial peers) are mitigated by context and opportunity – particularly in relation to social groups and networks. This is entirely consistent with the findings of Laub and Sampson (2003) in the developmental study of young offenders up to the age of 70 in which they emphasise the importance of events – particularly around the impact of work and relationships – in enabling desistance from offending careers.

The point is not that the events themselves force the change – there are many offenders and substance users who work and are married – but about the impact of these events on the values, beliefs, norms and the lived experience of the individual. That is why trajectories of change can be seen as the context in which trigger events can generate windows of opportunity for change. And this change will rarely happen overnight. For something to be a turning point, it has to have sufficient material and subjective impact to influence daily routines and practices but also the beliefs and values of the individual. As will be argued in the next section, there is a risk of over-stating good and bad biographical events (deaths, births, marriages, the gaining and losing of jobs and houses) and under-estimating the impact these things have on daily routines and on the social worlds that people live in. Within a developmental model, the individual has to have access to the resources to capitalise on windows of opportunities that appear, and also there have to be the prevailing contextual circumstances that allow suitable trajectories for the opportunity to translate into a sustainable turning point.

It makes sense that residential rehabilitation is a key turning point reported by many of the addiction professionals – and frequently cited by those in the Glasgow Recovery Study (Best *et al*, 2011a, b) – as it is a major life transition in routines and practices but also in the social world that the individual lives in for that period of time. In the online Melbourne sample, the primary example of this was engagement in mutual aid groups rather than formal treatment.

It is also why the therapeutic relationship is so important in underpinning the success of community treatment. For alcohol clients, Connors *et al* (1997) showed the independent effects of both worker and therapist ratings of the working alliance on active participation in treatment and drinking outcomes up to 12 months later. Horvath and Symonds (1991) had shown the importance of ratings of the therapeutic alliance, particularly the ratings made by clients, on treatment outcomes in a meta-analysis of psychotherapy, with the findings persisting irrespective of the therapeutic model used. What is crucially important about this finding is that the impact of the relationship – the interpersonal component – is likely to exceed the effects of the treatment itself. In other words, it is the human bind and link that may precipitate effective change among substance users in treatment. This is the fundamental social component within the developmental recovery model that transcends the treatment setting – in other words, it may happen in treatment, but it certainly does not have to.

As in the earliest recovery pathways study (Best *et al,* 2008), the trajectory of change involves two important social changes – moving away from the using network and the active engagement in a recovery network and community. Residential rehabilitation affords a clear window of time and space (rehabs are usually in geographically remote settings and contact with the outside world is limited and strictly controlled), so enabling the 'moving away from' the using network. However, it also offers a new social milieu including not only fellow residents but also the staff cohort which will typically contain a number of people in mature recovery. So the turning point that residential treatment offers in a recovery journey involves the practical component of physical separation from the using group for an extended period of time (of up to one year) but also exposure to a new set of activities, peers and values.

However, not all of those who attend rehabilitation succeed and, even among those who are successful, it is not always the first episode of treatment that will generate an enduring turning point in the transition to recovery. There are two further components that are needed to support the recovery pathway as shown in **figure 9.1**.

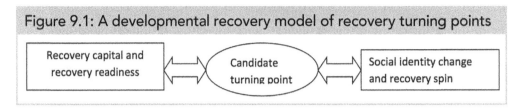

Figure 9.1: A developmental recovery model of recovery turning points

| Recovery capital and recovery readiness | Candidate turning point | Social identity change and recovery spin |

The basic hypothesis is that the client has to have a basic level of personal and social capital (or develop that very quickly) combined with a desire or motivation for recovery at the time the candidate turning point arises, whether that is treatment or not. If those conditions are in place, and if the candidate turning point (the window of opportunity for change) is embraced, a life trajectory change is possible. However, that initial turning point will only result in growing and emerging recovery if two further things happen – a significant change in the individual's social identity and social world, and the emergence of a 'recovery spin'. In other words, the initial change results in both lasting transitions in who the person sees themselves as being (mediated by social networks and social activities) and these activities generate the opportunities for further personal and social capital gains, that reinforce the initial changes. These ideas – social identity change and recovery spin – are outlined in more detail in the next two sections.

How turning points change the social world

Having reached this point in the book, you will be aware of the central importance attributed to social networks and social identity. The evidence is extremely clear that those who change their social networks have a significantly greater chance of achieving and sustaining abstinence and recovery from both alcohol and drug studies.

Decreased support for substance use (Longabaugh *et al,* 1998; Longabaugh *et al,* 2010) and increased support for sobriety from the social network (Litt *et al,* 2007) were each associated with reduced risk for relapse to alcohol use. Zywiak *et al* (2009) extended these findings to poly-substance use treatment, finding that decreased social support for drug use was positively associated with abstinence at six months post-treatment. The number of people in the network, the proportion of the pre-treatment network abstinent or in recovery (Zywiak *et al,* 2002) and the addition of abstinent and recovery friends most strongly predicted post-treatment outcomes (Mohr *et al,* 2001). So there is a strong evidence base from a range of studies showing the importance of changing social networks to recovery groups as an important predictor of long-term change.

In this model, there are two key influences on the rationale for this change – the first from Moos' work on the psychological mechanisms underpinning long-term recovery (Moos, 2007), in particular the ideas of social learning and social control, and second, the social identity model of identity change. From the Moos model, the idea is that people have to learn the techniques of recovery and that they do so by observing and copying the successful methods employed by the role models. This requires exposure to appropriate role models and the desire to emulate their achievements. However, spending time with such role models has a second effect – the incorporation of their norms and practices. In other words, spending time with people in recovery means abiding by their rules – and this has a practical as well as a psychological impact. Thus, spending time with a recovery group involves activities that will exclude drinking and drug use, as well as actively engaging in recovery activities. For our populations, engaging in mutual aid and other recovery groups, has the effect of altering the daily routines (and so reducing the exposure to substance risk) while also providing the values and beliefs and social supports for recovery values. But the impact of this form of social contact also involves the internalisation of the roles and values of the group. The 'social control' element of the Moos model is about the transmission of values that shape and constrict the individual's options for behaviour.

It is at this point that there is a strong overlap with, and role for, the social identity model. Based on the work of Tajfel and Turner (1979), from a social psychology tradition, the basic premise is that the self consists of both social and personal identity components and each of these will become dominant dependent on the context and situation the individual is in and the previous positive effects that this identity has resulted in. In a range of contexts, a person's sense of self is therefore defined by their membership of a range of social groups. Thus, group membership provides not only a sense of social support but access to a social lens through which the world can be understood. One of the origins of the social identity model, self-categorisation theory, also emphasised that the perception of oneself as a member of one social category or group involved excluding oneself from being a member of other groups or categories, such as active substance users (Turner *et al*, 1994). So those who identify themselves with a recovery group will therefore exclude themselves from the using group identity and so will be more likely to access a recovery identity in situations of risk for relapse and use.

The social identity model offers an explanation for how the recovery identity emerges – through exposure to attractive recovery role models and groups which promote social learning and imitation. However, increased exposure to the recovery champions or groups leads to the internalisation of the group's values and norms (Jetten *et al*, 2012), enabling the group to exert a form of social control that is accepted and internalised as part of the process of immersion in the group. Thus, within the developmental model, as the person gradually feels dissatisfaction with the using lifestyle and has a window of opportunity for change, the recovery group represents an alternative model if it is available and accessible. Residential rehabilitation or mutual aid groups both offer ready access to both the social networks and the individual champions of recovery. They are by no means unique in this respect but to deal with rehabilitation in particular, it offers that combination of a significant life turning point, access to recovery communities and individual champions of recovery and a structured and supportive environment that will provide the space and time to develop adequate recovery capital for the ongoing recovery journey. The role of the therapeutic community in particular is about learning 'right living' and its origins in communal growth and learning are entirely consistent in the social learning and social control model. The time spent in the TC setting is also a significant opportunity for growing the personal skills and building the social resources and capital for life beyond the TC.

The second example is around mutual aid group attendance, whether in conjunction with formal treatment or as a standalone pathway to recovery. This was widely cited in all three of the recovery stories outlined in previous chapters, with it frequently used as an alternative to or follow-up for formal treatment. In spite of considerable stigmatised views about 12-step groups among addiction professionals and many patients (Gaston *et al*, 2010), the 12-step fellowships are a global phenomenon that have assisted a huge number of people as evidenced in the three geographically disparate samples drawn from very different recovery populations. Yet 12-step engagement and active membership is a perfect example of how the social identity phenomenon arises. Humphreys *et al* (1999) have shown that the greater the levels of 12-step participation, the better the outcomes, and this can be conceptualised in terms of social identity change.

12-step membership is effective in part because of the social learning and social control, and the impact on values and beliefs (Moos, 2007) – newer members learn the ropes from 'recovery elders' through listening to their stories and hearing the methods and techniques that others have used to support their recovery journey. The notion of sponsorship is a particularly important one in 12-step groups and offers a form of mentorship to new members, but also binds more experienced members into the group. Within a social identity model (Jetten *et al*, 2012), alcoholics and addicts will often speak of 'hitting rock bottom' as what enabled them to start on their recovery journey and to engage with the mutual aid fellowship. At that point, the addict is identifying the failures that substance use have visited on their lives and so the 12-step group offers not only a source of social support but a social group where people who have been through the same thing have managed to overcome their problems and get their lives back.

Thus the initial application of the social identity model is around the attraction of the group – for the addict or alcoholic it offers hope that the substance can be overcome and access to a group with higher status and value than the former using group. The process of integration with the group is achieved through the internalisation of the group's values and norms and increasing self-categorisation as a member of the group (Tajfel & Turner, 1979). In turn engagement in the group results in the membership of the group becoming a lens through which the person comes to see the world – 'one day at a time'; 'fake it 'til you make it'; 'keep it by giving it away' that is linked to a sense of efficacy and belonging (Haslam *et al*, 2009). This is in part based on the research showing the benefits of social connectedness on general health and well-being (Putnam, 2000), but more about the benefits that a sense of belonging has in providing safety and protection to the individual in early recovery. While it is simplistic to say that the person who is at a 12-step meeting is not in the pub, if you have internalised the values and beliefs of a group who recognise that they should not spend time in pubs with fellow drinkers, and who construct activities and networks that do not include drinking, then it is possible that a high level of protection is afforded against the temptations of lapse and relapse.

An intriguing addition to the Social Identity Model has been suggested in a recent paper by Swann *et al* (2012) on the idea of 'identity fusion'. In contrast to traditional social identity theory, where aspects of personal or social identity have a better fit with the context or are more salient and so are utilised in responding, identity fusion would suggest that as individuals become strongly attached to and identified with particular groups, they come to become a dominant part of the person's identity and so fuse the personal and social components. 12-step group membership would be a candidate for this phenomenon, where regular engagement in activities – meeting attendance, doing service and so on – leads to a dominance of the steps and traditions, as well as membership of the group in identity.

What is crucial about the Social Identity Model as it applies to both therapeutic communities (and possibly other residential rehabilitation services and to mutual aid groups) is that it offers an explanation for the transition to recovery through processes of attraction, internalisation of recovery values and routines, and the generation of a new form of social identity that is both beneficial through access to support and opportunity and through providing a recovery lens for dealing with challenges of maintaining a recovery path. In the next section, the notion of recovery spin will build on this idea of sustaining change.

The recovery spin and 'stable recovery'

12-step is the common thread that unites the three sets of research findings presented in the current work. Alcoholics Anonymous and Narcotics Anonymous were widely cited and acknowledged by many of those involved in recovery. However, a model of recovery is not simply a model of 12-step group involvement because of the number of people – particularly in the Glasgow and Melbourne online samples – whose recovery did not involve mutual aid groups to any significant extent. Furthermore, among the addiction professionals, where some period of 12-step involvement is the norm, there remains a disparity between those who continue to engage in the groups and those who do not. Thus, the last section of this discussion is about what is common to the continuity of recovery pathways. This will rely on two concepts – the established notion of recovery capital and the linked but relatively new idea of recovery spin.

The notion of recovery capital rests on the resources that an individual can draw upon (Granfield & Cloud, 2001) and critically their link or bind to those resources. Although categorised in various ways, the three types of capital – which are overlapping and clearly dynamic in their evolution – are the skills and resources the person possesses (personal or human capital, sometimes also supplemented by physical capital) community capital and social capital. These domains not only overlap but they also interact and the developmental model is based on the notion that successful recovery is about a positive trajectory of recovery capital that emerges from the recovery turning point.

The example that illustrated this most clearly to me was the work done on the Second Chance sport programme in the northeast of England with repeat offenders who were involved in substance use (Landale & Best, 2012). In this initiative, participants were actively engaged in sport – primarily football – as a means of providing an alternative activity. But it did much more than that for them, as the young men started to develop a sense of pride in themselves (their physical health and well-being), in the team (involving a sense of belonging and a sense of commitment to the team) and an emerging sense of self-efficacy. In this way, the key personal qualities for recovery – self-efficacy, self-esteem and coping skills – emerged dynamically with the social effects of feeling a sense of positive identity in themselves and the team.

However, the other key point about the Second Chance model is that it also allowed a different kind of access to cultural capital through associating with different people and in a different context. The team opened doors to community opportunities including training courses, housing opportunities and jobs. This is precisely the kind of cultural capital (information and access) that Putnam (2000) regarded as central to social capital. It is not just who people know that matters, it is the connections that they afford to information and opportunity. Thus, the participant who did feel a sense of belonging and positive identity in the Second Chance programme had the positive physical capital of improved health and well-being reflected in improved performance in the team, generating self-esteem and a new identity that reinforced the incorporation of the group's values and norms, and so generating greater commitment to the group.

This is the basis for the idea of 'recovery spin' – while it makes sense to take a snapshot of personal recovery capital or social recovery capital to enable targeted interventions and support, the reality is that recovery spin will lead to a positive recovery trajectory through the dynamic growth of each of the key components of recovery capital. This is the critical component of the developmental model of long-term recovery transition that is implied in the work of White and Kurtz (2006) in their argument that stable recovery will typically take around five years to achieve after the recovery turning point. Developmentally, it is the trajectory that is experienced in this period – manifested as growth or stagnation and reduction in recovery capital – that will predict long-term recovery success. That is not to suggest that there is only one path to recovery but that, however common the triggers for starting the journey, and whatever the commonalities of the turning point itself, the recovery spin will vary markedly from person to person.

This recovery spin is usefully conceptualised as 'eudaimonia' or human flourishing. This is not a hedonistic model of happiness but rather it is the idea of living life well and being the best the person you can be. Many of the addiction professionals talked about 'giving back' and making a valuable contribution and this is key to the concept of recovery. Although the journey to recovery is an intrinsically social one, the paths on this journey become increasingly diverse as the shared beginnings of the recovery journey give way to divergent lives, albeit with a common theme of supporting and helping others to make the same journey.

References

Best D, Ghufran S, Day E, Ray R & Loaring J (2008) Breaking the habit: a retrospective analysis of desistance factors among formerly problematic heroin users. *Drug and Alcohol Review* **27** 619–624.

Best D, Gow J, Taylor A, Knox T, Groshkova T & White W (2011a) Mapping the recovery stories of drinkers and drug users in Glasgow: Quality of life and its associations with measures of recovery capital. *Drug and Alcohol Review*, early online.

Best D, Gow J, Taylor A, Knox A & White W (2011b) Recovery from heroin or alcohol dependence: a qualitative account of the recovery experience in Glasgow. *Journal of Drug Issues* **11** (1) 359–378.

Connors G, Carroll K, DiClemente C, Longabaugh R & Donovan M (1997) The therapeutic alliance and its relationship to alcoholism treatment participation and outcome. *Journal of Consulting and Clinical Psychology* **65** (4) 588–598.

Gaston R, Best D, Day E & White W (2010) Perceptions of 12-step interventions among UK substance-misuse patients attending residential inpatient treatment in a UK treatment setting. *Journal of Groups in Addiction and Recovery* **5** 306–323.

Granfield R & Cloud W (2001) Social context and natural recovery: the role of social capital in overcoming drug-associated problems. *Substance Use and Misuse* **36** 1543–1570.

Haslam SA, Jetten J, Postmes T & Haslam C (2009) Social identity, health and wellbeing: an emerging agenda for applied psychology. *Applied Psychology: An International Review* **58** (1) 1–23.

Horvath A & Symonds B (1991) Relation between working alliance and outcome in psychotherapy: a meta-analysis. *Journal of Counseling Psychology* **38** (2) 139–149.

Hser Y, Longshore D & Anglin M (2007) The life course perspective on drug use: a conceptual framework for understanding drug use trajectories. *Evaluation Review* **31** 515–547.

Humphreys K, Mankowski E, Moos R & Finney J (1999) Do enhanced friendship networks and enhanced coping mediate the effects of self-help groups on substance abuse? *Annals of Behavioural Medicine* **21** (1) 54–60.

Jetten J, Haslam SA & Haslam C (2012) The case for a social identity analysis of health and wellbeing. In: J Jetten, C Haslam & SA Haslam (eds). *The Social Cure: Identity, health and wellbeing* (pp3–19). New York: Psychology Press.

Landale S & Best D (2012) Dynamic shifts in social networks and normative values in recovery from an offending and drug using lifestyle (pp219–236). In: CD Johnston (ed). *Social Capital: Theory, measurement and outcomes*. New York: Nova Science Publishers Inc.

Laub J & Sampson R (2003) *Shared Beginnings, Divergent Lives: Delinquent boys to age 70*. Cambridge, Mass: Harvard University Press.

Litt MD, Kadden RM, Kabela-Cormier E & Petry N (2007) Changing network support for drinking: initial findings from the network support project. *Journal of Consulting and Clinical Psychology* **75** (4) 542-555. doi: 10.1037/0022-006x.75.4.542.

Longabaugh R, Wirtz PW, Zweben A & Stout RL (1998) Network support for drinking, Alcoholics Anonymous and long-term matching effects. *Addiction* **93** (9) 1313–1333. doi: 10.1046/j.1360-0443.1998.93913133.x.

Longabaugh R, Wirtz PW, Zywiak WH & O'Malley SS (2010) Network support as a prognostic indicator of drinking outcomes: the COMBINE study. *Journal of Studies on Alcohol and Drugs* **71** (6) 837–846.

Mohr CD, Averna S, Kenny DA & Del Boca FK (2001) Getting by (or getting high) with a little help from my friends: an examination of adult alcoholics' friendships. *Journal of Studies on Alcohol* **62** (5) 637–645.

Moos R (2007) Theory-based active ingredients of effective treatments for substance use disorders. *Drug and Alcohol Dependence* **88** (2–3) 109–121.

Putnam R (2000) *Bowling Alone: The collapse and revival of American community*. New York: Simon and Schuster.

Shover N (1985) *Aging Criminals*. Beverley Hills: Sage.

Swann W, Jeten J, Gomez A & Whitehouse H (2012) When group membership gets personal: a theory of identity fusion. *Psychological Review* **119** (3) 441–456.

Tajfel H & Turner J (1979) An integrative theory of intergroup conflict. In: W Austin & S Worschel (eds). *The Social Psychology of Inter-group Relations* (pp33–47). Monterey, CA: Brooks/Cole.

Thornberry T, Freeman-Gallant A, Lizotte A, Krohn M & Smith C (2003) Linked lives: the intergenerational transmission of antisocial behaviour. *Journal of Abnormal Child Psychology* **31** 171–184.

Turner J, Oakes P, Haslam S & McGarty C (1994) Self and collective cognition and social context. *Personality and Social Psychology Bulletin* **20** 454–463.

White W & Kurtz E (2006) The varieties of recovery experience. *International Journal of Self Help and Self Care* **3** (1–2) 21–61.

Winick C (1961) Maturing out of narcotic addiction. *Bulletin on Narcotics* **14** (1) 1–7.

Zywiak WH, Longabaugh R & Wirtz PW (2002) Decomposing the relationships between pretreatment social network characteristics and alcohol treatment outcome. *Journal of Studies on Alcohol* **63** (1) 114–121.

Zywiak WH, Neighbors CJ, Martin RA, Johnson JE, Eaton CA & Rohsenow DJ (2009) The important people drug and alcohol interview: psychometric properties, predictive validity, and implications for treatment. *Journal of Substance Abuse Treatment* **36** (3) 321–330. doi: 10.1016/j.jsat.2008.08.001.

Chapter 10: Recovery and the future

This final chapter outlines some of the key directions for research and policy that derive from the theory and findings presented earlier in the book. A theory of addiction recovery that fits with the evidence presented has been outlined, but there is insufficient evidence to enable firm conclusions to be drawn, and the theory is open to empirical falsification. In other words, there are clear hypotheses that can be derived from the conceptual model that will allow it to be tested. As suggested in Best (2012) there is a general paucity of adequate research about recovery pathways and the aim would be to outline a research agenda that maps personal journeys to recovery. However, that is only the first objective, and there is also a clear need to 'translate' some of these suggestions about research to implications for practice and for policy – sections 2 and 3 of this chapter address these questions and concerns. In section 4, the chapter will examine wider questions about the future directions of the 'recovery movement' in the UK and internationally, and the final section of the chapter will provide an overview about some of the key emerging issues about the application of research models to practice.

What do we need to know about the science?

The call for more research is a familiar refrain from researchers and this researcher is no different, but in this case there is a very strong policy imperative for greater recovery-focused research and that relates to the greater focus of policy-makers on recovery and their attempts to translate the principles of recovery to routine practice.

At the level of individual recovery change, as stated in previous chapters, there is considerable evidence about the effectiveness of formal treatment with a basic pattern showing that sufficient retention and adequate treatment engagement leads to significant improvements across a range of treatment modalities – the evidence for this comes from outcome studies such as the NTORS study in England (Gossop *et al*, 2003), the DORIS study in Scotland (McKeganey *et al*, 1996) and the TOPS study in the US (Hubbard *et al*, 1989) for drugs and Project MATCH (Project MATCH Research Group, 1998) and the UK Alcohol Treatment

Trial (UKATT Research Team, 2005) for primary alcohol problems. The strongest work in this area has been done by Laudet (eg. Laudet & White, 2008) with a New York based follow-up study of people early in recovery who were tracked prospectively with a focus on predictors of well-being and quality of life, but this model needs to be developed and extended.

In spite of the evidence of treatment effectiveness, relatively little is known about the effectiveness of aftercare other than that it generally significantly enhances the effects of treatment (White, 2007). There is a major omission around identifying the types and durations of appropriate aftercare and how they are linked to involvement in mutual aid. For recovery journeys to be considered in terms of a period of approximately five years beyond acute treatment (Betty Ford Institute Consensus Group, 2007), then it is critical that much more research effort is spent on understanding the support needed at different stages of the recovery journey and how this might vary by personal circumstances and by personal recovery goals. The next section will also focus on the question of the therapeutic alliance and what the worker can do to enable and support recovery pathways.

It is noticeable that, as indicated in Chapter 9, the research on addiction careers is significantly behind that undertaken in academic criminology where there has been much greater investment in research that is longitudinal and over sufficient time to map long-term change pathways and their likely causes. Thus, the work by LeBel (2008) in this area has re-evaluated the Laub and Sampson (2003) analysis to question the causal impact of jobs and relationships on desistance from offending. The question LeBel (2008) posed was whether relationships and jobs are markers of internal change rather than causes – in other words, that individuals need to have sufficient recovery capital already before such structural changes are likely to be significantly protective. A similar question arises for the impact of meaningful activities in addiction recovery and it is crucial that we start to develop an understanding of the dynamics of change if we are to develop a science of recovery.

The developmental question that arises from this study is the concept of recovery spin and the idea that there are cumulative benefits that can create a spiral of recovery success for individuals. The notion of a spiral of personal and social recovery growth requires much more research investigation and this will also necessitate a much better understanding of the links between personal and social capital. In this book, I have argued that there is a complex dynamic between personal and social recovery capital and to investigate this will require a different kind of research that requires much more regular and routine monitoring. There is also no reason to assume that this is a linear growth process and it may well be the case that the overall trajectory of change is much more unstable. However, mapping recovery capital – and linking it to both recovery identities and visibility – will be a major area for study.

Our own work is only now beginning to explore the concept of social identity and how this changes over time – in line with the model developed by Jetten *et al* (2012). The assumption that is made here is that recovery necessitates a social support system – both as a replacement for the using group and as a source of support and resources. However, it is additionally beneficial if at least some of this group is in recovery as this affords the opportunity for learning the techniques of recovery but also developing a 'recovery social identity'. We still have relatively little idea of what that means and how that emerges or manifests in terms of other aspects of personal or social identity. It is also not clear how the prominence of recovery identities grows and changes, and the circumstances under which, for at least some people, recovery identity diminishes as they move beyond a recovery identity as a salient part of their personal and social world. Therefore, there is a major prospective piece of research required that maps changes in social identity over time and that tracks the ebb and flow of recovery as a salient social identity and how that links to personal and social recovery capital.

This is particularly important in the context of recovery champions where the social identity of recovery is likely to be highly salient, and where there may both be positive and negative consequences of high visibility. Indeed, 'recovery champion' is a term that some people have expressed unease about as it implies a status that may place too many demands on the individual. The professionals included in the main study here partly address this question, but there is a wider question about the transition from early to stable recovery and then on to being identified and acting as a recovery 'elder' or 'champion' that we know very little about – or what the levels of functioning, support or need are in this group. Particularly in the UK, where the role of champions is enshrined in policy, there is a significant responsibility being placed on people relatively early in their recovery journey. Thus, there is an urgent need, to ensure their needs are protected and their recovery supported and enhanced, that we do more to investigate who they are and how the role of champion affects their well-being and growth. This issue will be addressed in more detail in the section 'Communities and policy' but for the next section attention will turn to the key emerging research questions from this work around the role of workers and treatment services.

There are three questions that I set out to address in this book that the data and the analysis do not provide sufficient grounds for adequate consideration. They are:

1. Gender differences in recovery pathways: There is a strong impression from the data – particularly the online recovery stories – that the experiences of men and women in recovery are systematically different. This is a key issue for recovery services but not one that can be answered here. There may also be equivalent differences by ethnic and cultural groups, and by age, but again, this must be the subject of future study.

2. Cultural differences in recovery experiences in the UK and Australia: Because of the different attitudes to recovery in Australia (where many professionals and experts are more overtly hostile) and the UK, I had anticipated that there would be marked differences in openness in talking about recovery. That was not the case and this may reflect the sample – those who took part were those who are open about their recovery.

3. Context and climate: The book has talked at length about the social ecology of recovery and the community and context effects that can both support recovery (through vibrant and visible recovery communities) and that can suppress recovery (through stigmatisation and discrimination). This is a huge subject, with enormous ramifications for policy and practice, and will be the focus of my work moving forward.

Treatment and interventions

As outlined in Best (2012), there are differences in standard treatment and recovery-oriented treatment that relate to orientation and focus. In a recovery-oriented model, the worker has four key roles:

1. to help overcome the acute physical and psychological problems that will prevent engagement in recovery activities

2. to provide a sense of hope and belief that recovery is possible – in other words to be a human catalyst for recovery

3. to support the development of personal recovery capital through engagement in therapeutic activities and to provide continuity of care and support

4. to provide bridging capital to link the person in with social groups and activities that can promote the ongoing recovery journey.

We are still early in the process of articulating the components of effective recovery-oriented practice in the AOD field, although Sheedy and Whitter (2009) have gone some way to outlining some of these key components, including a personal and respectful relationship and the perception of the therapeutic relationship as a partnership. Within a developmental recovery model, providing the belief that recovery is possible and providing adequate linkage to recovery groups and champions is central to the idea that the worker can act as a relational turning point, if they provide belief in recovery and have an enduring and supportive relationship that enables effective linkage and guidance.

One of the core areas of study here is around the worker as a core part of 'helping capital' (Cheong *et al,* 2013). This area of study investigates the role of professionals (in this case, pharmacists) as resources that the individual can draw upon to address their illnesses (in the original research this was around asthma). In my work on recovery, numerous stories involve reference to at least one worker who 'went the extra yard' in supporting the recovery journey and who provided a sense of hope and inspiration. It is critical that this extended and revised notion of the therapeutic alliance is understood in recovery terms and part of that process is to map the role that a range of professionals can play in the recovery journey, in their roles as 'therapists', as links to recovery groups and communities and through the relationships that emerge with the person in recovery. The assumption of the recovery model is that recovery is a social developmental process and for the development of recovery-oriented working practices it is essential that we have a better grasp on what makes a worker inspirational and engaging. This also has significant implications for training and professional development.

Of course, many of these workers may well be in recovery themselves although that is not a prerequisite. Professionals represent a huge candidate army of recovery champions if they are willing to commit to active engagement in the community and moving beyond the professional role to one of advocate and to be a part of the community, outside of the workplace and working hours. The current work starts the process of research inquiry into the population of workers who are themselves in recovery, but this is such a critical population and significantly more work is needed to understand their pathways and to understand the roles they play. The issue addressed in this book around the risks faced and experiences of being open about recovery requires considerably more work, as this group are critical to the idea of recovery contagion.

This provokes a more generic question about the supports and needs of recovery champions – including but not restricted to those in the professional alcohol and drug workforce. There is a major piece of work to do to identify their needs and to provide them with adequate supports – and this is something that does not appear to be addressed adequately at the moment within the UK system. This group have to manage their own risks and well-being while also supporting others and creating support systems for champions and mechanisms for identifying their support, training and development needs is both a workforce and a research question that urgently needs to be addressed.

There is also a considerable literature that shows that assertively linking clients into mutual aid groups not only improves engagement (Timko *et al,* 2005) but also that they significantly benefit in terms of their outcomes (Manning *et al,* 2012). However, this emerging evidence has not been applied outside of AA in a systematic way and similar models need to be developed for other forms of assertive linkage into other key pathways to recovery – including community and sports groups, education and employment, volunteering and peer support. There is a major opportunity for developing assertive linkage skills as a core part of the workforce development of professionals and of peer champions. The professionalisation of addiction services in the last 20 years in both the UK and Australia has meant that there is an increasingly desk-bound culture among workers in community treatment services and this is not consistent with the idea of effective linkage and involvement in the community.

This will also necessitate improved measurement of worker attitudes to recovery and active engagement in recovery processes, and learning from the mental health recovery movement about adequate workplace competencies and attitudes will be a major step forward. There will also need to be increased coverage of recovery in vocational and academic courses for addiction professionals to provide the basic knowledge and skills and reconciling that with an academic model that has a strong commitment to empowering and skilling up people in recovery for champions roles. These are major challenges that require both development and evaluation.

Communities and policy

There has been increased interest in the idea of asset-based community development in drug policy particularly in the UK (eg. ACMD, 2013) but this has not been translated into the notion of a reciprocal responsibility to communities. Thus, a question that is more of an audit question than a research one is the contribution that treatment and recovery services make to their lived communities, including but not restricted to the staff, clients and graduates. The notion of asset-based community development should be a reciprocal one in which the agency, its staff and its clients make a contribution to the lived community and engage in activities that support that community, rather than simply regarding the local community as a kind of larder to be raided as part of the client's 're-integration' journey.

The same principle applies to assertive linkage, whether to mutual aid agencies or wider in the community – the agency has a responsibility to ensure that the clients are as prepared and ready as they can be and that people who are referred will not be a significant risk to themselves or others. Assertive linkage cannot be a one-way street with recovery or treatment services referring clients indiscriminately. One of the key questions for clinical research around recovery is around assessment and preparation of individuals to assess their suitability for engaging with different types of groups and providing both preparation and support to the individual through mentoring and effective and personalised bridging. However, the service must also act as a hub for community linkage by developing contacts and connections in each candidate agency and supporting the agency to receive the new clients. For this relationship to have sustainability, all parties must benefit and all parties must be active participants in the process – this should be co-produced community enhancement.

One of the consequences of such a co-produced benefit should be a challenge to stigmatised and discriminatory attitudes in the community. Stigma and discrimination are fundamental barriers to recovery by both socially excluding individuals identified as problem users (Braithwaite, 1989) and by acting as a barrier to social identity and social contagion. The primary communities of recovery have either been isolated by anonymity (the 12-step fellowships) or by geographic isolation (rehabs and in particular the therapeutic communities) and it is only in recent years in the UK and the US that there has been some attempt to create a visible recovery community.

One of the arguments advanced by White (2007) is that a primary method of challenging and overcoming stigma is through direct exposure to people in recovery – challenging stereotyped and pejorative views. The recovery movement – through political lobbying, through celebratory walks, and through a range of community engagement activities – has gone a long way to establishing a positive face for recovery. In my own work, in Barnsley, the establishment of a recovery coalition of peers, professionals and other members of the community, led to a dynamic growth of a range of activities that promoted and supported recovery activities (Best *et al,* 2013). The visible presence of a recovery community provides clear opportunities for challenging stigma by providing clear evidence of community and success; but it also challenges internalised stigma among active and recovering addicts by witnessing not only recovery success (and thus providing access to social learning) but also through creating a positive categorical social identity (ie. recovery is a viable social identity that is worth striving for). Those who are part of successful public recovery events not only are bound more strongly to the group but also witness the effective integration of recovery with everyday activities. In Barnsley, the Lord Mayor's Parade, the sports day and the recovery walk were all events that create a high visibility for recovery, that is supported by a cross-section of the community and that creates high social reinforcement.

This is even more the case for events that support the community – in the UK these include tidying up the riverside, clearing snow from drives and houses, and a diverse array of community supports and activities. These events are crucial in that they enact recovery not only in a positive light but illustrate that recovery groups can constitute community recovery assets that in turn can create bridging capital. However, there is almost no research on the impact of such activities on the sense of recovery identity among groups and individuals; of the type of activities that serve this purpose or their effects on community stigma and discrimination.

For the purpose of the current model, the other key research question that arises is about the impact of the emergence of a visible recovery community on the social contagion of recovery. This is a measurable research question. If successful community events take place, the commitment of visible recovery champions to a social identity of recovery should be enhanced (through both categorical and relational social capital) but there should also be fewer community barriers to engaging in recovery activities. In other words, the impact of successful community recovery events should be fewer active barriers in the community (through bridging capital and increased exposure to recovery among the general public) but also by reducing the internalised barriers to engaging in recovery communities and activities among those in active addiction or early recovery who observe or learn about successful recovery events.

This is a major challenge for establishing recovery as viable social policy where reintegration to families, workplaces and communities is a fundamental goal – and indeed intrinsic to the definitions of recovery. Breaking down both negative attitudes and actions in the community and the related internalised stigma beliefs and experiences is essential (and open to measurement) and is a fundamental goal for recovery research and policy. While there are national strategies and activities that can contribute, this is fundamentally a local question of tracking visibility and recovery contagion as it relates to changes in community attitudes and structural barriers to recovery.

Future directions of the recovery movement

The recovery movement is as complex and as difficult to pin down as recovery itself. The most obvious manifestations of the recovery movement has been around the number of 12-step groups, SMART groups and alumni or aftercare groups linked to recovery-oriented treatments such as rehabilitation services and therapeutic communities. However, the emergence of the more ambitious recovery umbrella organisations who have acted as political pressure groups – particularly Faces and Voices of Recovery in the US and UKRF and RGUK in England – has led to a different model for understanding and measuring recovery communities and the 'recovery movement' in a way that is intrinsically different from similar experiences in mental health or other equivalent disciplines.

One of the obvious risks is that the recovery movement becomes mainstream – and this is most obvious in England where some of the most prominent critics of recovery and who have done the most to block the objectives of recovery – have been given leading roles in policy groups around recovery, and have explicitly attempted to reconcile recovery with acute treatment. The watering down of the recovery model is not inevitable but requires a commitment to grassroots change and a fundamental paradigm shift in addiction policy, treatment and science that takes the key expenditures and activities out of the hands of vested interests, professional bodies and opportunistic and cynical careerists. Recovery is intrinsically about connections and community capital and any attempt to return it to the domain of the professional and the clinic should be resisted in favour of celebrating the genuine achievements of recovery.

A final comment: the application of recovery to practice

Recovery is normal but recovery is remarkable.

As illustrated in this book, based on very different populations and locations, recovery is something that lots of people achieve and they do so in an incredible diversity of ways, yet each one of these is worth celebrating. Addiction is tenacious and pernicious and so those who do overcome it are typically remarkable people, although they may not have been when their journey started. The evidence is mounting that recovery is a process of personal growth that typically is supported and sustained by others in the peer group, the family and the community, and that leads to a reserve of resources – personal and social – that creates real assets in the community. It is our ability to support and sustain those assets and, where possible, enable them to transmit the social contagion of recovery, that will ultimately decide the success of the recovery movement.

References

Advisory Council on the Misuse of Drugs (2013) *What Recovery Outcomes Does the Evidence Tell Us We Can Expect? Second report of the recovery committee*. London: ACMD.

Best D (2012) *Addiction Recovery: A movement for personal change and social growth in the UK*. Brighton: Pavilion.

Best D, Loudon L, Powell D, Groshkova T & White W (2013) Identifying and recruiting recovery champions: Exploratory action research in Barnsley, South Yorkshire. *Journal of Groups in Addiction and Recovery* **8** (3) 169–184.

Betty Ford Institute Consensus Panel (2007) What is recovery? A working definition from the Betty Ford Institute. *Journal of Substance Abuse Treatment* **33** 221–228.

Braithwaite J (1989) *Crime, Shame and Reintegration*. New York: Cambridge University Press.

Cheong L, Armour C & Bosnich-Anticevich S (2013) Primary health care teams and the patient perspective: a social network analysis. *Research in Social and Administrative Pharmacy* http://dx.doi.org/10.1016/j.sapharm.2012.12.003.

Gossop M, Marsden J, Stewart D & Kidd T (2003) The National Treatment Outcome Research Study (NTORS): 4-5 year follow-up results. *Addiction* **98** 291–303.

Hubbard RL, Marsden ME, Rachal JV, Harwood HJ, Cavanaugh ER and Ginzburg HM (1989) *Drug Abuse Treatment: A national study of effectiveness*. Chapel Hill, NC: University of North Carolina Press.

Jetten J, Haslam SA & Haslam C (2012) The case for a social identity analysis of health and wellbeing. In: J Jetten, C Haslam & SA Haslam (Eds). *The Social Cure: Identity, health and wellbeing* (pp3–19). New York: Psychology Press.

Laub J & Sampson R (2003) *Shared Beginnings, Divergent Lives: Delinquent boys to age 70*. Cambridge, Mass: Harvard University Press.

Laudet AB & White WL (2008) Recovery capital as prospective predictor of sustained recovery, life satisfaction, and stress among former poly-substance users. *Substance Use and Misuse* **43** (1) 27–54.

LeBel T (2008) The chicken and egg of subjective and social factors in desistance from crime. *European Journal of Criminology* **5** (2) 131–159.

Manning V, Best D, Faulkner N, Titherington E, Morinan A, Keaney F, Gossop M & Strang J (2012) Does active referral by a doctor or 12-step peer improve 12-step meeting attendance? Results from a pilot randomised control trial. *Drug and Alcohol Dependence* **126** (1–2) 131–137.

McKeganey N, Bloor M, Robertson M, Neale J & MacDougall J (1996) Abstinence and drug abuse treatment: results for the drug outcome research in Scotland study. *Drugs: Education, Prevention and Policy* **13** (6) 537–550.

Project MATCH Research Group (1998) Matching alcoholism treatments to client heterogeneity: Project MATCH three-year drinking outcomes. *Alcoholism: Clinical and Experimental Research* **22** (6) 1300–1311.

Sheedy CK & Whitter M (2009) *Guiding Principles and Elements of Recovery-Oriented Systems of Care: What Do We Know From the Research?* HHS Publication No. (SMA) 09-4439. Rockville, MD: Center for Substance Abuse Treatment, Substance Abuse and Mental Health Services Administration.

Timko C, Dixon K & Moos R (2005) Treatment for dual diagnosis patients in the psychiatric and substance abuse systems. *Mental Health Services Research* **7** (4) 229–242.

UKATT Research Team (2005) Effectiveness of treatment for alcohol problems: findings of the randomised UK Alcohol Treatment Trial. *British Medical Journal* **331** 541–544.

White W (2007) Peer-based recovery support systems. Pittsburgh, PA: Northeast Addiction Technology Transfer Center, Great Lakes Addiction Technology Transfer Center, Philadelphia Department of Behavioral Health & Mental Retardation Services.

White W, Evans A & Lamb R (2009) Reducing addiction-related social stigma. *Counselor* **10** (6) 52–58.